Lines, Tines & Southern Pines

Discovering Life through Fishing, Hunting and Outdoor Tales

Corey W. Jenkins

Copyright

Copyright © 2016 by Corey W. Jenkins. All rights reserved. Written permission must be secured from the publisher or author to use or reproduce any part of this book, except for brief quotations in critical reviews or articles.

Author: Corey W. Jenkins
Editor: Greg McElveen
All photos except where noted: Copyright © 2016 Corey W. Jenkins
Cover photographs: Copyright © 2016 Drew Senter
Formatting: Greg McElveen
Proofreading   Kathy Phipps

Library of Congress Control Number: 2016949797
Library of Congress subject headings suggestions:

1. GV191.2-200.66   Outdoor life - Outdoor recreation
2. SK650-664   Wildlife-related recreation
3. SK40-268   Hunting Sports-By Country – Southeastern United States

BISAC Classification Suggestions:

1. BIO023000 BIOGRAPHY & AUTOBIOGRAPHY / Adventurers & Explorers
2. SPO030000 SPORTS & RECREATION / Outdoor Skills
3. SPO014000 SPORTS & RECREATION / Fishing
4. SPO022000 SPORTS & RECREATION / Hunting
5. SPO002000 SPORTS & RECREATION / Archery

ISBN-13 for Black and White Paperback: 978-1-937355-39-5   V: 1.0
ISBN-13 for Color Hardback: 978-1-937355-38-8   V: 1.0
ISBN-13 for eBook: 978-1-937355-40-1   V: 1.0

To purchase additional copies of *Lines, Tines & Southern Pines* or to learn more about the author go to his author page on Amazon.com or visit: www.linestinespines.com or go to Big Mac Publisher's website: www.bigmacpublishers.com

Big Mac Publishers, Kingston, TN 37763
Written and processed in the United States of America

Lines, Tines & Southern Pines

Quotes, from respected Reviewers

"Corey Jenkins has crafted a set of stories that will have you crying, laughing and begging for more. Told with folksy humor and down home charm, *Lines, Tines & Southern Pines* belongs on every person's bookshelf that enjoys experiencing the outdoors with friends and family."

***Robert Bailey**, Author of "The Professor" and "Between Black and White" *

"This is the top book in this genre I've read in years. I chuckled out loud, and even wiped a tear during some touching scenes. The crazy tales are mindful of Huckleberry Finn on steroids. Corey's style is transparent, fluid, comical, and genuine. He is the kind of guy I'd like to meet. His book is absolutely a delight for all ages, male and female. There are some rather intriguing fishing and hunting episodes, but the true emphasis is on relationships, fun, and insights about lessons learned in the outdoors."

***Rocky McElveen**, Master Guide/Owner, Alaskan Adventures and Author of the top selling "Wild Men, Wild Alaska" books *

"Lines, Tines & Southern Pines is subtitled 'Discovering Life through Fishing, Hunting and Outdoor Tales' which aptly defines it. Mr. Jenkins leads us through a youth spent largely in the woods or on the water searching for the beast of a lifetime. Instead he discovers life's lessons that the great outdoors has taught young men and women for generations. A fun and easy read that led me down a path of nostalgia where I laughed right out loud and shed tears as I remembered fondly the teachings of my own parents and grandparents. The stories are entertaining and thought provoking as you realize that relationships with the people in your life are sweeter and richer having shared such experiences."

***LePage Ward Owens**, Retired Teacher, Real Estate Broker*

"Jenkins' tales are heartfelt and comical. He is the perfect blend of Bill Heavy and John Gierach. *Lines, Tines & Southern Pines* is a must read for the Southern outdoorsman."

***Drew Senter**, Oxford, Alabama, Founder: Longleaf Photography*

"I remember reading the story of a commercial airline pilot whose copilot asked him why, on one of their regular routes, he always looked down and sighed at the same place on a tiny river each time they passed over it. He replied that when he was a small boy he would be sitting down there on a log, fishing, when planes would fly over, and he would wish with all his heart that he were up there flying the plane. But now that he was grown and flying, all he wished for with all his heart was that he could be that small boy again, back down on that log fishing. For anyone who loves the outdoors and craves to go back and be that small boy or girl again, reliving the joy and innocence of a blessed childhood well lived in the outdoors with loved ones now gone, Corey has stories that will take you back in your mind to those times in your life, and bring smiles to your face, and maybe tears to your eyes."

***Steve Hacker,** Florence, Alabama, www.smallmouth.com*

"When my brother said, 'Sis, you gotta read this book.' I retorted that I didn't like fishing and hunting books that showcased men's prowess or boring techniques. He laughed and said I was in for a real treat. Oh My Goodness! I loved it. It was not about harvesting fish or animals, but written from a kind heart, a fun-loving prankster, and a real man who involves his wife, daughters, friends, and now his readers in such interesting stories. Corey is not afraid to be transparent, or display his foibles and his wit will catch you off guard. As others have noted, I too cried and immensely enjoyed his humor. As I read, I was right there with him, visualizing the scenes, seeing the beauty of nature, and reveling in the craziness. Ladies, buy this for yourselves, then give it to your hubby!"

***Ginger Hammons**, Happily Retired, Kingston, Tennessee*

"This book sparks so much emotion. I don't know if I laughed more, or cried more, but I did a good bit of both. I was thoroughly entertained by each and every story, and once I picked it up I didn't put it down until I finished. It is appropriate for (almost) all ages and has some good lessons on family, friendship, life and how to respect life. This collection of short stories will make anyone from Alabama (especially North Alabama) proud."

***Sunshine Calvin**, Huntsville, Alabama*

Table of Contents

Copyright iv
Table of Contents v
Introduction vii
The Outdoors to Me (in 100 words) xi
1   My First Catch 1
2   Traditions 7
3   Scarhead 17
4   The Refuge 27
5   Doe Fever 31
6   The Cove 37
7   Not Anymore 49
8   Patches 55
9   The Hangup 61
10 The Grill and the Road 67
11 The Fishing Nut 75
12 Charlie 2 Shot 83
13 One of Those Days 97
14 Pass the Sausage 105
15 My Girls 115
Acknowledgments 139
About the Author 141
Glossary: Understanding the Local Lexicon 145

"Many men go fishing all of their lives without knowing that it is not fish they are after."

Henry David Thoreau

Introduction

Writing a book became a life goal of mine at the age of fifteen. I was first inspired after rolling out of bed just before noon on a Saturday in July after a long night of Zelda, Mario, and other video games. As soon as I mustered the energy to make my first appearance of the day, I came to the unfortunate realization that I was home alone and would have to fend for myself for breakfast.

After scouring the kitchen for something to eat, I decided that the last Sara Lee microwave dinner in the freezer would test the extremes of my culinary skills. I eagerly ripped opened the red box without any regard for instructions, tossed the frozen dinner in the microwave, set the timer for thirty seconds, and pressed Start.

A few moments later, I jumped at the "Ding" of the microwave, tore open the clear plastic cover of the dinner, and attempted to eat the first mouth-watering bite, which was still completely frozen. The frustration was overwhelming as I added additional time to the microwave numerous times to cook the dinner throughout. After several minutes, I finally plopped down at the kitchen table to enjoy an exotic Sara Lee dinner for breakfast.

As I sat at the kitchen table eating breakfast and contemplating life through the lens of a daydreaming fifteen-year-old, I realized that I absolutely had to write a book. The decision to write a book had nothing to do with literary aspirations, although I did read a lot of Mark Twain, Ernest Hemingway, *Bassmaster*, and *Buckmasters*. It also had nothing to do with drive, determination, or passion, which I generally reserved for fishing, hunting, video games, sports, and Jimmy Buffett music.

I decided to write a book because, as I sat at the table eating a Sara Lee microwave dinner, I had a random thought that starting a book with a guy sitting at a table eating "exotic Sara Lee" would immediately be a bestseller. I had no doubt that the book would be enjoyed by millions of people and would change the landscape of writing for generations.

Later that day and numerous times over the next few years, I started writing a book with a guy sitting at a table eating "exotic Sara Lee." I never made it past the first page. At some point, I came to the unfortunate realization that the idea wasn't quite as good as I had thought. That, or the execution was bad. Regardless, I eventually abandoned the idea of writing a book using the phrase "exotic Sara Lee."

The inspiration to write a book hibernated through a few decades and a lot of life, including many of the stories included in the following stories. During that time, I said goodbye to PawPaw and lost my childhood dog and companion, Casper. I also realized that my best friend was the love of my life and asked her to be my wife. Together, we later welcomed two beautiful daughters into the world. Between earning several degrees, moving numerous times, working, spending time with family, and living life, the idea of writing a book became a distant dream from childhood.

A few years ago, a friend and colleague of mine that founded Huntsville Outdoors approached me and asked if I would consider writing a piece about hunting in North Alabama. After considering it for a few weeks, I reluctantly agreed and decided to write "The Refuge," a story about the Wheeler Wildlife Refuge (or the Refuge as I've always called it) and a few memories and adventures on the Refuge.

After I finished The Refuge and sent it to Huntsville Outdoors, the founder called and said he really enjoyed the story and was going to post it. He also told me that he was surprised by the story, specifically because it didn't involve killing anything. I laughed and told him that, at least to me, hunting, fishing, and the outdoors are about much more than killing animals and catching fish.

A year or so after writing The Refuge, several friends of mine and I were sitting around a table sharing outdoor experiences at a hunting lodge. I ended up telling one of the stories that follows in the upcoming pages. As soon as I finished the story, a good friend commented that I should write short stories of my outdoor experiences to share with others. I laughed at the suggestion and dismissed the idea.

Earlier this year while sitting in church with family, an overwhelming inspiration hit me, and my life goal to write a book came roaring out of hibernation. The inspiration wasn't just to write a book, it was to write a specific book about hunting and fishing experiences in the outdoors. I have never been one to ignore an inspiration (especially one in church) or not to follow my gut, which brings me to today and this book.

I firmly believe that time and experiences in the woods and waters kept me out of trouble during the younger years of my life and shaped and molded the person that I am today. Without doubt, life would have been extremely different had I not been introduced to the outdoors at a very young age and been given the opportunity to experience and enjoy the outdoors. For this reason, I try to introduce as many people as possible to the woods and waters that I love so much and that are so much a part of me.

Every hunter, fisherman, and outdoorsman has stories about his or her experiences in the outdoors. The following stories are a few of mine. I truly hope that you enjoy reading them as much as I enjoyed living them, reflecting on them, and putting them down on paper.

The Outdoors to Me (in 100 words)

I have always loved the outdoors. My girls share the same love, and I could not be prouder. In the outdoors, I reflect on the past and look to the future; I smell the wind, taste the sun, and feel the energy around me as I wait for a deer to approach or a fish to bite (and not caring if they don't); I feel close to God and those who have gone before me; and I am the most *me*. I can relax and breathe in the outdoors. The outdoors are and will always be a part of me.

Corey W. Jenkins

Love of fishing started early for me

1
My First Catch

From the time I could walk and talk until I turned six, I would exclaim, "I AM FOUR!" whenever someone asked, "How old are you?" I pretended to be many things as an imaginative child, including four. There wasn't anything magical about four – it was just my favorite number for some unknown and random reason.

During the several years when I was four, I often saved the galaxy from the dark side, trained to play football for the "Bear," fought pirates while hunting for treasure, and hid beside the cross ties under the plum tree in the back yard while waiting to hear the screaming of the worn belts on Dad's old brown Ford as he turned into the driveway so I could scare him and hopefully convince him to join me on an adventure.

Dad worked on the railroad throughout my childhood. The work was difficult and the hours were long, especially with the overtime he worked on nights and weekends to provide for our family. Even though he was often gone, Dad always found or made time for our family. While I truly cherished every second I spent with him as a child, I will never forget one special afternoon with Dad in late summer when I was four.

I was desperately trying to save mankind in an epic space battle beside the closet in my bedroom when I was startled by the loud creaking of our old red back door opening. Mom was in the other room, and it was too early in the afternoon for Dad to be home. I sat in the floor petrified with terror strategizing on how to defend and protect the house, especially the toys, from the intruder until I heard Dad yell, "HEY COR!"

Relieved, I jumped up, ran through the room dodging the toys in the floor, and hurdled through the door jamb onto the faded vinyl floor in the kitchen, just barely missing Dad. He was standing by the back door grinning when he looked down at me, grabbed my shoulder, and asked, "Do you want to go fishing, Bud?"

I had always fantasized about joining Dad on a fishing trip and could not believe that the dream was actually coming true. I immediately yelled, "YES!" For the first time, at four, I felt like a man and could not have been prouder or more excited.

Dad had filled the minnow bucket and the cricket tube, packed snacks, and taken care of everything for our adventure. We told Mom and my sister Sunni bye and took off to a spot Dad had found near Crybaby Holler on Flint Creek that was a short walk off of the railroad tracks down a gravel bank.

My excitement grew with each passing second as we drove to the fishing hole. I jabbered the entire way and was ready to pop when Dad finally put the Ford in park on the gravel path. As soon as the dust cleared, we jumped out, unloaded the car, and started walking down the railroad tracks toward the creek.

Dad carried all of the gear as I balanced on the rails and scanned the area for pirates. When we finally arrived at the steep gravel bank, Dad somehow held me, the minnow bucket, the crickets, a Zebco rod and reel, and the rest of our gear as we slid down what felt like a rock mountain to our fishing hole.

Dad spent the day showing me how to fish, which consisted primarily of skipping flat rocks, catching dragonflies, and fending off pirates. It was *my* day, and Dad did everything he could to make and keep me happy. He showed the patience of a saint and didn't mind that we weren't catching fish, which was likely a result of me scaring away every fish in a ten-mile radius.

The blue sky was showing hints of the violets and oranges of dusk when Dad turned to me and said, "Get ready for the last cast." With Dad's help, I baited the hook with a cricket and made a cast downstream just past the point where the creek bent to the right.

The ripples on the surface had just settled when the red and white bobber bounced slightly and then ripped to the left. Dad scrambled to help me set the hook and then coached me through the fight. I screamed with excitement as the fish tested the limits of our equipment and my fishing skills at four.

After a long and draining fight, Dad stepped into the edge of the creek and landed the small bream. I will never forget the look on his face when he turned, held up my first catch, and said, "Good job, Son." I will also never forget the deep and complete pride, excitement, and satisfaction that I felt after catching that first fish and making Dad proud.

Dad showed me how to hold the fish and take the hook out of its mouth while standing by the creek as the sun disappeared for the day. He then patted me on the back and said, "Let's let him go."

Through all the excitement, I had not realized that Dad was planning to release the fish. I unsuccessfully attempted to hold back the tears as I looked up at Dad and pleaded, "Dad, can't we keep it?" Dad explained that the fish was too small to eat and that we needed to release it. Devastated, all I could do was stand on the bank of the creek and cry.

My emotional pleas to keep the fish eventually changed Dad's emphatic "No" to an "OK, Son." We put the bream in the minnow bucket to keep him alive and headed back to the brown Ford to go home.

When we arrived home that evening, everyone made a big production about the fish. I wanted the night to last forever. When Mom asked, "What are we going to do with your fish," I immediately responded, "Can we put him in the bathtub… please?"

Mom and Dad looked at each other with concern and skepticism and discussed whether to put the fish in the bathtub. After begging, "Please Mom" and, "Please Dad" for some time, they reluctantly agreed to fill the bathtub in our small bathroom with water so the fish could swim around.

I sat by the edge of the bathtub watching the fish swim when I looked back at Mom and Dad and asked, "Can I keep it as a pet?" Mom and Dad attempted to gently tell me no, but I wouldn't stop the pleas until I was given a good reason. Mom lightly patted me on the back in the way only a loving mother can and said, "I'm sorry, Baby, but you can't keep the fish because the water is too dirty."

The tears that only a four-year-old can cry poured out at the realization that I couldn't keep the fish because the water was too dirty. Mom and Dad left me in the bathroom with the bream to say goodbye. I was furious, devastated, and heartbroken that the water wasn't clean enough for the fish.

As I sat on the floor between the toilet and the bathtub staring at the fish, grieving, and coming to terms with the loss of the fish, the realization that all I needed to do to save the fish was clean the dirty water hit me like a ton of bricks. I scanned the bathtub and the rest of the bathroom desperately looking for something to clean the water. I was about ready to give up when I looked up and saw the answer to my problem.

I nearly hit my head on the underside of the porcelain sink when I jumped up to grab the bottle of Dawn dish soap sitting on the edge of the sink. I figured that if Dawn could clean dishes, it could also clean the water, allowing me to keep the bream forever.

I proceeded to dump the entire bottle of Dawn in the bathtub and turned on the water. Mom and Dad came running into the bathroom when they heard the water running and me shouting.

To their surprise, the bream had gone from swimming in a tub to floating upside down in a bubble bath. They simultaneously asked, "What happened?" I looked up at Mom and Dad and said in an exasperated and confused tone, "I cleaned the water with the Dawn soap to save the fish, but something went wrong."

Mom and Dad ran out of the bathroom as quickly as possible. At the time, I thought they were figuring out how to revive the bream. I found out later they had left so I wouldn't see them laughing.

That evening, we buried the bream beside the cross ties under the plum tree in the back yard. It was an emotional night to say the least. I shed many tears under that plum tree, both that night and later as other beloved pets joined my first catch.

As I sit here many years later, I can still smell Dad's old brown Ford and hear the screaming belts that needed replaced. I can still see the drooping fabric on the roof, the microwave in his back seat, and the mismatched golf clubs and tools in his trunk. I can still feel the wind in my hair as we drove down the road with the windows down, which was necessary since the air conditioner never worked. I can still remember the pride and excitement that I felt because Dad took me fishing when I was four. I will never be able to thank him enough.

Thanks to Dad, my love for fishing was born next to a creek alongside railroad tracks in North Alabama when I was four. On the same day, I also experienced my first loss and learned how not to clean water. Most importantly, Dad taught me at four the fulfillment of spending time with others in the outdoors and the importance of making time for your children.

Passing along Dad's lessons to El Brooke

2
Traditions

Hunting season is a time-honored and long-standing tradition in Alabama. From the time I could walk, I wanted to wear camouflage, shoot guns, and join my cousin Steve during hunting season, particularly at the annual hunt at noon on opening day of dove season in September.

A few weeks before the opening day when I was five, Steve stopped by the house to see the family and play Atari. After a short visit, Steve shoved me, messed up my hair, and dodged my wild punches as I tried to get him back.

As he was laughing at me and dodging every swing, he asked, "Are you going to hunt with me on opening day this year?" I was frozen by Steve's question and looked at Mom and asked in my saddest and most pitiful tone, "Can I please go?" After considering Steve's question and my pleas, Mom, in her stern and authoritative voice, said, "You can go as long as Steve promises to take care of you and if you promise to be very careful."

To say I counted the seconds to opening day would be a gross understatement. After Mom agreed to let me go hunting with Steve, I wore camo around the clock and didn't talk about anything other than hunting. By the time morning of opening day rolled around, I couldn't contain my excitement any longer.

I stood by the door holding the Daisy BB gun Santa had brought me the year before and wearing the same camouflage I had slept in the night before waiting on Steve and my grandfather PawPaw to arrive. Around 10:00, they finally pulled into the driveway. As soon as I saw them, I threw the door open and ran into the driveway ready for my first hunting trip.

Mom told me to wait up as she followed me out the door. After a few quick pictures, Steve, PawPaw, and I took off for the annual opening day tradition.

PawPaw, Steve and me

A few minutes after we arrived at Steve's old red house, other trucks started arriving for the opening day hunt. By 11:00, everyone that was there to hunt was standing in Steve's front yard eating amazing barbecue pork sandwiches from Southern Hickory Barbecue in Hartselle and sharing laughs, jokes, and stories from seasons past.

Around 11:45, we all split up to head to different areas around the large dove field. I went to the best spot on the property with Steve and PawPaw.

Hunting with PawPaw

We spent the remainder of the day sitting in a torrid field for hours on end listening to Alabama football on the radio, playing fetch with Steve's lab, Bear, joking with each other, waiting for birds to fly, and, except for Steve (who has always been a crack shot), generally just barely missing if and when the birds flew over. Words cannot express how big and important I felt sitting on a green bucket between Steve and PawPaw on my first hunt.

Throughout the day, Steve and PawPaw worked with me on proper shooting form and emphasized the importance of gun safety. I took countless shots that day at fence posts, rocks, cans, and bottles. The doves, however, were safe.

Throughout the hunt, I begged and pleaded with Steve and PawPaw to let me shoot their shotguns. They both generally let me try and get away with anything, but neither was willing to let me shoot his gun. They both insisted that I was too young and small and that I would get hurt by the kick of a shotgun, although it likely had more to do with the fact that Mom would have turned the barrel on them had anything happened to me.

At the end of the day, Steve asked if I wanted to hunt with him opening day of the next hunting season. Excitement overwhelmed me as I emphatically screamed, "Yes!" I was now a part of the tradition, and I was counting the days until opening day the following September.

As promised, 364 days later I was sitting in front of Steve's red house eating pork sandwiches from Southern Hickory Barbecue, feeling like a man, and preparing for the hunt. I had graduated from a pump Daisy BB gun to PawPaw's pellet rifle, but what I really wanted to shoot was Steve's shotgun.

Preparing for opening day

I started begging to shoot Steve's gun before the season kicked off and continued begging throughout opening day. Steve held firm, but the annoying pleas were slowly chipping away at his nerves and resolve.

Finally, toward the end of the afternoon, Steve succumbed to my charm, perseverance, and annoyance and asked, "Do you really want to shoot my shotgun, and will you stop whining if I let you shoot?" I eagerly confirmed both and reached to grab his shotgun. Steve laughed at me, pulled back his gun, and told me that I could only shoot his shotgun if I learned how it worked and then only if I did it correctly.

For the next several minutes, Steve showed me the ins and outs of his shotgun, including how to use the safety, how to load and unload a shell, how to shoulder it, and how to aim. I impatiently insisted that I understood each of the lessons and begged for him to let me shoot the gun. Steve finally agreed and reluctantly handed me the shotgun.

I was tall for a six-year-old, but only slightly taller than Steve's 12 gauge. I utilized every bit of my strength to lift the shotgun to my shoulder. Unfortunately, my young muscles just weren't strong enough to lift and shoulder the gun and shoot it.

Steve knew that I was extremely disappointed. He encouraged me that I would be big enough to shoot his shotgun the following year and promised that he and I would shoot together the next opening day.

Steve could not have handled the situation any better, but I wasn't quite ready to give up. I turned to Steve with a tear in my eye and asked him in the most heartbroken and manipulative tone, "Can I sit down and shoot?" Steve reluctantly agreed and helped position me for the shot.

I kneeled down, planted my right knee on the ground, rested my left elbow on my left knee, and straightened my back. Steve then handed me the gun and told me to aim at the tree just ahead of us.

The weight of the gun was nearly unbearable, but I somehow mustered the strength to hold up the shotgun. I held the butt of the gun firmly on my young and inexperienced shoulder, rested the bead at the end of the barrel on the tree, and leaned over to rest my cheek on the stock in preparation for the shot.

Steve frantically yelled, "STOP!" and told me not to rest my face on the gun. He then explained the difference between shooting a BB gun and shooting his shotgun and emphasized the importance of not resting my cheek on the gun. I dismissed Steve's suggestion and told him I understood.

My pride and satisfaction reached an all new high as I prepared to shoot Steve's shotgun. I once again braced the butt of the gun to my shoulder, raised the barrel, rested the bead on the tree, and laid my face on the gun. Again, Steve stopped me and yelled, "Don't put your face on the gun!" Steve's tone finally convinced me to listen, and I told him I understood and wouldn't do it again.

For the third time, I locked the butt of Steve's shotgun on my shoulder, raised the barrel, and held the bead on the tree in front of me. This time, however, I kept my face off of the gun and told Steve I was ready to shoot.

Steve reached down and helped me flip the safety to fire, stepped behind me, and said, "Shoot when you are ready." My muscles ached from the weight of the gun as I tried desperately to steady my nerves and hold the shaking bead on the tree.

I looked up to Steve, and the last thing I wanted to do was miss the tree and disappoint him. I followed the exact process Steve had showed me: I kept the butt of the stock firmly on my shoulder, I held the gun just as Steve had showed me, I controlled my breathing, I held the bead on the tree, and I slowly squeezed the trigger and felt the explosion of Steve's shotgun.

The gun went off without a hitch. Unfortunately, I had laid my face on Steve's 12 gauge the moment before I pulled the trigger. I understood that the kick to my shoulder would potentially hurt a little. What I had missed during my lessons was that the kick of the shotgun to my face would feel like a knock-out punch from a heavyweight boxer. I learned that lesson the hard way as I flipped backwards several times with a busted nose and what quickly turned into two black eyes.

As I lay on the ground staring at a hazy sun through tear-filled eyes, Steve stood over me shaking his head, and exclaimed, "I told you not to lay your head on the gun." He then rushed me home to Mom.

A new and important tradition was started the afternoon I was punched in the face by the kick of a 12 gauge. I have never again laid my face on a shotgun.

The opening day tradition changed over time, but without fail, I was in the field continuing the tradition every opening day until I left for college twelve years after being nearly knocked out by Steve's shotgun.

As a result of school, a hectic schedule, and life in general, the opening day traditions eventually faded and turned into fond memories from the past.

Our oldest daughter is now the same age I was when Steve's shotgun nearly broke my face. From the time she could walk, she has always wanted to wear camouflage and shoot and hunt with her daddy.

While teaching her how to shoot a gun last year, I couldn't help but laugh when I told her not to rest her face on the gun. She immediately pulled her head back and shot correctly. Thankfully, she listens a lot better than me.

I have promised her that she and I will start hunting together this year, and I recently cleared a field for us to start our opening day tradition. Good Lord willing, we will be eating pork sandwiches from Southern Hickory Barbecue at 11:00, heading to our field just before noon, and spending time together laughing and enjoying the outdoors on opening day this September.

I just hope she doesn't ask to shoot my shotgun.

Dada, can I shoot your gun!?

Daddy, can I please shoot your shotgun?

3
Scarhead

Mom's father, Dude, or PawPaw as I always called him, had a way with names. The names he came up with were usually based upon a trait, fact, or characteristic that was typically obvious. I am confident PawPaw was never accused of being creative in the naming department.

He eloquently named a calf that had hurt its neck and could only walk in circles with his head stuck sideways on his shoulder "Crook." I'll never forget the family dinner where PawPaw announced, "I hope the steaks are good – we're eatin' Crook." His proclamation was followed by grunts, sighs, the sound of forks dropping on plates, and several colorful comments. It didn't bother me – Crook was delicious.

PawPaw also had a beautiful stark white calf that he named based upon the color of her head. For whatever reason, the calf's mother had abandoned her at birth. Every time the calf came near, the mother cow would either run away or try to charge or kick the calf.

The calf needed its mother's milk, so it tried desperately to nurse. Eventually the calf started sneaking behind its mom and nursing between the mother's back legs. This would generally work for a few minutes before the calf received a manure bath. After several failed attempts at nursing, the calf's white head permanently turned a shade of mustard brown. PawPaw affectionately named the calf "Shithead." Shithead was our favorite cow.

Shithead, our favorite cow

PawPaw's names weren't just limited to cows. For example, he called Mom "Baby" until the day he died, which was logical since she was his youngest child. He would also generally introduce me as his "Baby's baby" (which also made sense because I am in fact Mom's youngest child).

PawPaw had names for just about everything. However, I only remember one catfish that he deemed worthy of a name.

PawPaw had a small catfish pond on the back of his farm. After a long day of work in the summer, we would often ride out to the pond to feed the catfish and, if I was lucky, throw his old Zebco rod and reel in hopes of catching enough catfish for dinner, or a "mess of catfish" as PawPaw would always say.

PawPaw loved his catfish and made sure they were well fed. I believe PawPaw's catfish ate better than he and his family had eaten during the Great Depression.

When we threw feed in the pond, the catfish would always come to the top, and he would point out the ones that he recognized. We always looked for one specific catfish that had a scar down the left side of her head that he had named "Scarhead."

PawPaw feeding his fish

I never understood PawPaw's fascination with Scarhead, but I always shared it. I loved looking for Scarhead and seeing PawPaw's excitement when she made an appearance.

A few years before he died, PawPaw purchased another small farm that was a half mile or so up the gravel road from his old farm house. The farm was perfect for cattle and hay, but it was missing a catfish pond. PawPaw didn't need much encouragement before he decided to build a pond on the new farm.

PawPaw brought in large equipment to build his perfect catfish pond, which he wanted to be twelve to fifteen feet deep beside the dam with a slow transition to the shallow creek and standing timber. After the pond was dug and before it had water, I spent many days in the hot July sun with PawPaw picking up every single rock from the bottom of the giant hole to make sure that our hooks didn't get hung.

To make the work easier, I would often sit down in an area within reach of several rocks and throw them out while sitting. One afternoon as I sat at the bottom of the pond throwing out rocks, PawPaw looked at me and joked, "You are the only man I've ever known that could work on his ass!" We had a good laugh over the comment but immediately went back to work.

PawPaw left me with the rocks and went to take Red Tractor (as eloquently named by PawPaw) to check something at his barn. An hour or so later, as dusk was approaching, I heard his tractor just over the hill. As I sat at the bottom of the large hole that would later become a pond, I looked at the top of the pond bank as PawPaw drove by. PawPaw and his tractor were little more than shadows in front of the vivid orange and indigo sky. The view took my breath away, and tears unexpectedly came to my eyes as I sat there and relished the moment. I can still see PawPaw riding Red Tractor on the edge of pond bank that afternoon. It still takes my breath away and brings tears to my eyes.

After a summer of rock removal, PawPaw decided that his perfect catfish pond was ready for water and catfish. The pond was not completely filled with water until that fall. After it was full,

PawPaw stocked the new pond with fingerling catfish. PawPaw also wanted to move a few of the catfish from his other pond. He said he was speeding up the stocking process, but it really seemed that he only cared about catching and moving one catfish, Scarhead.

We fished several days that fall to stock the new pond. We would put whatever catfish we caught in an old black tub in the back of his Ford truck and take them to the new pond. Each time we released the fish in the new pond, he would say that we needed a few more. I will never forget the look in PawPaw's eyes and the grin on his face when he finally caught Scarhead, lifted her proudly at the edge of the pond, and exclaimed, "Look at what I caught," then gently put her into the black tub. After transferring her into the new pond, he said that we had enough fish and declared that the pond was finished. I was eager to fish in the new pond the next spring with PawPaw.

Our new pond

PawPaw was always an ageless superhero, working from daylight to dusk every day and never seeming to tire. For the first time the next spring, PawPaw seemed old and fragile.

PawPaw called me on a Thursday afternoon in spring and asked if I could help him till his garden the upcoming weekend. I always loved spending time with PawPaw and eagerly agreed to help.

I drove to PawPaw's house first thing the following Saturday morning to spend time with him and help him with his garden. After working for less than an hour, PawPaw asked if we could take a break and talk. PawPaw's idea of a break generally consisted of taking a quick drink while walking briskly to do something else, and only then after finishing what you were working on. I didn't know what to think about him wanting to stop before we finished his garden, but I was excited to spend time with him, just the two of us.

For the next several hours, he and I sat at his oak kitchen table and talked about many things we had never discussed: his childhood, the war, the untimely death of his infant son, and how proud he was of me. When PawPaw hugged me that afternoon, he held on longer than usual. For the first time, I worried about PawPaw.

PawPaw was sick throughout most of the spring and summer. He would occasionally have a day where he felt well, but those days were rare and were generally followed by several consecutive bad days.

I was sitting in class in October when one of my favorite teachers, Ms. Smith, pulled me out of class to tell me that Dude was sick and had been taken and admitted to the hospital. I immediately walked out of school without checking out and drove to the hospital.

When I arrived at the hospital, I ran to the front desk to ask for PawPaw's room number and hurried to the elevator. When I stepped off the elevator on PawPaw's floor and turned the corner, I saw PawPaw in a wheelchair being pushed by a nurse. I walked over to him and asked, "How are you PawPaw?" Prior to that day, every time I had asked PawPaw how he was doing, he always responded, "I believe I'm gonna make it." This time, as he struggled to lean forward to hug me, he said, "I don't believe I'm gonna make it this time."

I felt like someone had hit me in the gut. I shook my head and told PawPaw not to be silly and that I would see him back in the room after the tests were finished. For the first time, I knew that my days with PawPaw were numbered. I kept a straight face until the elevator doors closed behind PawPaw. As soon as he was out of sight, I leaned back on the wall beside the elevator, slid to the cold floor, and cried as I sat in the hallway.

I stayed with PawPaw at the hospital every day he was there. Over the weekend, PawPaw took a turn for the worse and quickly declined. The doctors told us there was nothing more that could be done and that we should say our goodbyes. PawPaw had been non-responsive for some time when I finally gathered the strength and courage to go and tell him "Thank you" and "Goodbye."

I was sitting on the right side of his bed and holding his hand with my head on the side of his bed crying and praying when I felt a slight squeeze. Convinced I was imagining things, I looked up at PawPaw and saw that his eyes were open. He gently squeezed my hand, shook his head, whispered "Don't cry," pointed up to heaven, mouthed "I love you," and closed his eyes.

PawPaw passed away the following afternoon, on October 23. At the time, I was a sixteen-year-old kid who thought I knew everything. As I watched PawPaw take his last breath, I realized how little I knew, how much I had learned from PawPaw, and how much I was going to miss him.

That night, as I sat in the bed struggling with the loss of PawPaw, Casper, my dog and childhood companion, sat on the porch outside of the window howling and crying. As soon as I stepped on the porch to check on him, Casper, an eleven-year-old lab with bad hips, walked to me as fast as he could to lie beside me. I'm not sure which of us held the other, but I cannot imagine that night without Casper.

The next morning, I spent time alone with pen and paper to write about PawPaw. That paper turned into the eulogy that I read at his funeral. I haven't written about PawPaw again until now.

I awoke with a heavy heart a few days after PawPaw's funeral, on my birthday. PawPaw had always made a point to see me on my birthday and give me a hug. That morning, all I wanted was to see and hug PawPaw. Feeling lost and not knowing what else to do, I decided to spend the day alone at PawPaw's farm and hopefully feel close to him.

While driving toward PawPaw's farm, lost in thought and emotion, I had an overwhelming urge to take a detour down the county road to the cemetery. As I stood by the freshly dug grave praying and talking to PawPaw, I gazed at the sun, which had just peaked through the clouds, and closed my eyes to feel the warmth on my face. When I opened my eyes, I was mesmerized by a doe standing on the other side of the road looking at me. As I stood there watching the majestic animal, I was blinded by my tears. I looked down to wipe away the tears. When I looked up, I saw a white tail when the doe ran toward the woods. As the doe disappeared in the trees, I felt somewhat at peace for the first time in several days.

I have visited the graves of PawPaw and Granny at the same spot many times since that day. I have never seen another deer.

As soon as the doe disappeared into the woods, I left the cemetery to drive to PawPaw's farm. When I pulled in the gravel drive, I decided to go the new pond, our pond. I filled a five-gallon bucket with catfish feed and took off up the gravel road. I hoped to catch a mess of fish for my birthday dinner and maybe see Scarhead one last time.

I was shocked and disappointed when I did not see a single catfish after dumping the first cup of feed in the pond. I hoped that the fish were just deeper or not hungry yet, and made a cast to one of the holes that PawPaw and I had dug out the previous year.

The chicken liver at the end of the line sat on the bottom all morning without a bite. I eventually threw the entire five-gallon bucket of feed into the pond, all without seeing Scarhead or any other catfish. I had a good laugh thinking about what PawPaw would have said to me for wasting an entire bucket of feed when the catfish weren't hungry.

I was about to pack up and leave when I saw the line twitch for the first time that day. I grabbed the rod, pulled back gently, and, as soon as I felt weight on the line, set the hook fiercely. After a few minute fight, I pulled the fish onto the bank.

When I looked down at the fish, I noticed a scar along the left side of her head. Emotions came pouring over me when I realized I had caught Scarhead. I sat there on the edge of the dam that I had helped PawPaw clear and cried as I held PawPaw's favorite catfish, the only one he had ever named.

Through the tears, I couldn't help but smile. For the first time since I met PawPaw outside of the elevator at the hospital, I felt completely at peace.

If I could choose one meal as my favorite or my last, it would be fresh catfish from PawPaw's pond served on his old aluminum picnic table, and maybe fresh watermelon that we "borrowed" from his neighbor and best friend. I had set out on my birthday hoping to catch one last mess of fish from PawPaw's pond. As I sat there holding Scarhead, I knew that I wouldn't be eating catfish for dinner. Instead, I set up Mom's camera to take a picture of Scarhead and me by the pond, thanked Scarhead and God for letting me see her one last time, gave a nod to the heavens, and released Scarhead. I never saw her again.

Scarhead

Every year on my birthday, I spend time alone in the outdoors and reflect back on PawPaw and that day. I still miss PawPaw terribly, but I am comforted by the fact that I will see and hug him again down the road and hopefully reflect on Scarhead, wherever she may be.

4
The Refuge

There is a point at the end of every summer where you can feel a certain crispness in the air. The days are getting shorter, and the leaves on the trees are starting to show a hint of brown. This time of year signifies a number of things to me: football, crankbait fishing on Guntersville, chili, and last but definitely not least, bow hunting. Without fail, the first morning when I feel the crispness in the air, I think back and smile on my younger years deer hunting with friends on the Wheeler Wildlife Refuge, or "the Refuge" as my friends and I have always called it.

The Refuge is approximately 35,000 acres of woods, swamps, creeks, and farmland around the Tennessee River between Huntsville and Decatur, Alabama. While you can absolutely take deer from the Refuge with practice, time, and patience, hunting on the Refuge is about much more than deer. Many of my fondest memories growing up revolve around the Refuge.

Every summer, we would spend countless hours shooting thousands of shots with our bows in preparation for the upcoming season on the Refuge. In the afternoons, we would often drive gravel roads on the Refuge around Muscle Camp in Somerville looking for deer or, if it ever got too hot, swimming in the river.

In late September, we would start walking through the woods looking for the perfect spot to hunt. We referred to this tradition as "going scouting," even though we usually hunted the same areas each year, which were always the best in our eyes. Without fail, before sunrise on opening day of bow season on October 15 (or, if the 15th was a Sunday, the next day), we would walk to our favorite trees with treestands on our back, bows in our hands, and grins on our faces. After opening day, we would spend as much time as possible hunting and scouting on the Refuge.

Ben and me getting ready to hunt

Every year, we would see multiple deer while hunting, and we would generally have several opportunities to shoot. The vast majority of the time, we would decide not to shoot for one reason or another. At the time, we would say it was because the deer was too small, that we didn't want to drag the deer to the car, that we didn't really want to skin the deer, or that we wanted to save the spot for the next hunt. Looking back, I now realize that our hunting traditions were really about friendship, comradery, and memories much more than hunting.

In fact, the memories that I treasure most do not even involve taking a deer. I recall explaining to state troopers at 4:30 AM that we were *not* out drinking; waking up a friend in his treestand to tell him that he could have shot a large eight-point buck that walked right under his tree had he stayed awake; trying to fit our stands and hunting gear in my friend's small two-door Saturn; skipping the homecoming bonfire to hunt; trying to sneak back into school in full camo to grab my friend's hunting backpack; and watching the sun rise over the river a few days after my grandfather passed away and feeling close to him as the fog lifted. These memories are more meaningful to me than any deer I could ever shoot.

We all left North Alabama after graduating from high school. After leaving, we would often talk about getting back together to hunt the Refuge. For the first few years, we were able to occasionally meet to continue the tradition on weekends and holidays. However, as time passed and obligations and priorities changed, it became more and more difficult to coordinate schedules, and the Refuge became a fond memory from our pasts.

Several of us have now migrated back to North Alabama with our families. A few years ago, I was having lunch to catch up with a dear friend that spent the most time with me on the Refuge growing up. After reflecting on our favorite memories on the Refuge, we decided that we were way past-due for a trip to the Refuge.

A few hours later, we were walking down an old and familiar gravel road toward one of our favorite ridges where we used to hunt. Being that we were both more interested in reminiscing on the past than hunting, we decided to sit together that day to enjoy the outdoors and the company. After sitting less than twenty minutes, two deer walked out and stood less than twenty yards from us. We both immediately grabbed our bows and prepared to shoot. We both ended up watching the deer instead of shooting.

Apparently, we thought it was better to save the spot for our next hunt, whenever it may be.

5
Doe Fever

There is no adrenalin rush that compares to the feeling when a deer walks out and you prepare for the shot. It is a feeling that you cannot understand unless you have experienced it. You forget the cold, your hands sweat, your entire body shakes, and your heart beats so hard and fast that you are convinced the deer will hear it. The feeling is commonly referred to as "buck fever," and it is contagious and addictive.

I will never forget the first time I had a deer in bow range and was preparing to shoot. I was hunting on the Wheeler Wildlife Refuge in an oak bottom next to a bedding area. I had scouted the bottom earlier in the year and knew that deer frequented the area. I could not wait to get in the stand and hunt the spot for the first time.

I arrived to the tree well before sunrise on a Saturday morning. I attached the Summit climbing stand to the tree, tied a tow rope to my Hoyt bow with a three arrow quiver, and began the climb. I locked the climbing stand to the tree at about twenty-two feet, pulled up the bow while trying to be quiet and avoid tree limbs, and sat down to settle in and watch the fog lift and the world materialize with the sunrise.

The conditions were perfect. The wind was blowing directly in my face and the river, which had been several hundred yards away earlier in the year before the wet fall, was now approximately thirty yards from me and created a pinch point that would hopefully bring a deer within bow range.

I was sitting in the stand enjoying the sunrise through the fog and watching the woods come to life when I noticed movement to the right. My heartbeat went from docile to frantic as a large doe materialized from the fog about forty yards away on the edge of the water, and she was walking toward me. I quietly grabbed the Hoyt bow and stood up in preparation of the shot.

The few moments it took the doe to step in range felt like hours. With each step, my heart rate increased and my breath shortened. It was an adrenalin rush unlike anything I had ever experienced. The first case of buck fever I ever experienced was for a doe, and it was severe. I was convinced that the doe would either hear my heartbeat or see me shaking, but she had no idea I was there.

When I made the decision to shoot, time came to a crawl. I grasped the bow like I had done thousands of times in the back yard, connected the release to the string just under the arrow, bent my knees slightly, drew the string back slowly and, as the wheels broke, touched the string to my nose, held the nock of the arrow just under the corner of my mouth, anchored my right thumb to the back of my neck, and looked through the peep site. I then settled the second pin just behind the doe's front left shoulder as she stood broadside at twenty yards.

I tried desperately and unsuccessfully to regulate my breathing and calm my nerves. I took a deep breath and exhaled half way as I tightened the movement of the pin on the doe's shoulder. I slowly moved my right finger to the trigger of my release and squeezed. I will never forget watching the white feathers on the Easton aluminum arrow spin as the arrow approached the doe.

I had followed my exact process, made what felt like a perfect shot, and I knew the shot would hit, which is exactly what it did.

Unfortunately, what it hit was the tree several feet behind the deer. I missed the doe. The shot wasn't even close.

When the arrow hit the tree, the doe jumped, ran about forty yards, and then looked behind her. The doe was now out of range, and I could only watch her slowly walk away as the sight of the arrow sticking out of the tree haunted me.

I was upset, but also thrilled that I'd had the experience. Everything had gone exactly as I had hoped and planned, except the shot was horrendous. I had blown my first opportunity to shoot a deer with a bow on public land, and opportunities were rare.

I nocked another arrow hoping that the doe would magically turn around, walk back, and stand broadside at twenty yards again. I knew better.

As I sat in the stand reflecting on the terrible attempt at a shot, I saw movement to the right. Two young does walked out at the exact same place where the first doe had appeared. The does both angled to the left and, if they continued on their path, would walk less than twenty yards in front of me.

I had a relapse of doe fever as I slowly grabbed the bow and went through the exact same process. My heart was beating out of control as the doe stood there at fifteen yards slightly quartering away.

The situation was perfect, and I was able to somewhat calm my nerves. I once again settled the pin on the doe's shoulder, squeezed the trigger on my release and made the shot. I will never forget the arrow burying in the ground after flying several feet over the doe. I missed again. I missed again badly.

The missed shot scattered the two does. The doe that I missed, the one in front, ran to the left along the same trail as the first doe I had missed. The second doe ran back to the right where all three deer had appeared.

While I was thrilled to have seen the deer, I was devastated at the two shots. I had missed two golden opportunities to harvest my first deer with a bow on public land.

I decided then that the hunt was finished and stood up, turned to face the tree, and prepared to climb down. As I was adjusting the safety harness, I heard the sound of leaves rustling behind me.

I turned around and saw that the third doe had hesitantly walked out on the same trail again. I could not believe my eyes. Redemption shots and mulligans are rare in bow hunting, and the third opportunity was walking toward me. I grabbed the third and last arrow from the quiver, silently nocked it, and turned to draw back on the deer.

For the third time that morning, I drew the bow and settled the pin just behind the shoulder of a doe standing between fifteen and twenty yards from the tree. While I was once again suffering from a terrible case of doe fever, I was able to focus on the shot and somewhat regulate my nerves. I released the arrow with confidence and certainty.

I can still hear the thud when the arrow hit. The arrow flew straight and penetrated deeply. Unfortunately, the arrow flew straight over the doe's back and penetrated deeply into the ground.

I felt horrible. I had blown an opportunity of a lifetime three times in the same morning. I had missed the first doe I ever shot at with a bow, and then proceeded to miss two more the same morning. I had shot every arrow in my quiver, and none of the shots had even been close.

In a one hour period, I had gone from an extreme and unforgettable high to a deep and dark low three separate times. I didn't know what else to do but climb down, grab the arrows (while leaving one broadhead in a tree), and head home disappointed.

I replayed the shots countless times over the next twenty-four hours. On one hand, my confidence had been crushed, and I now questioned whether I was cut out for bow hunting. On the other hand, the thrill was unlike anything I had experienced, and I was hooked. That day, I became a bow hunter, albeit a very bad one.

A few days after I missed three does in one morning, I decided to start practicing again to make sure I didn't miss the next time. I placed the old foam target from Wal-Mart next to the hill in the back yard, stepped off twenty yards, grabbed the bow, connected the release to the string just under the arrow, bent my knees slightly, drew the string back slowly and, as the wheels broke, touched the string to my nose, held the nock of the arrow just under the corner of my mouth, anchored my right thumb to the back of my neck, and looked through the peep site. I steadied the second pin on the middle target and gently squeezed the trigger on the release.

The arrow flew several feet over the target and buried in the hill. For the first time since before the hunting trip, I looked closely at the bow sight and noticed that something was wrong. The screws on the sight bracket were a little loose and the sight had dropped, probably when I was walking to the woods or towing the bow up the tree. Regardless of when it happened, I was immediately relieved to know that I was not at fault for the missed shots. My confidence was back after I grabbed an Allen wrench, re-adjusted the sight, and was back to hitting quarters.

However, after two shots, the realization that the missed shots were absolutely my fault hit me like a ton of bricks. I should have checked the screws before the hunt and verified that everything was correct in the treestand. In the excitement and anticipation for the hunt, I had not checked my equipment and had paid the price.

Since that day, I regularly check and tighten the screws on my bow. I also check the bow every time I sit in a stand. I will be prepared the next time I sit in a treestand in perfect conditions and three unsuspecting deer walk by me at a perfect angle. Unfortunately, I know that it will likely never happen again.

I learned a lot the morning I experienced doe fever three times in one hour and shot out my quiver. Most importantly, I realized that there is no rush that compares to the thrill of bow hunting. That morning, I became a lifetime bow hunter.

Lifetime bow hunter

6
The Cove

The seed for my love of the outdoors was planted at a very young age. While my affinity for the outdoors grew with each childhood fishing and hunting trip, it truly flourished in a small slough on the lower end of Guntersville that I have always simply referred to as the "Cove."

Dad's mom and her husband George owned a small, run down, and virtually abandoned cabin at the very back of the Cove. Dad and I were visiting with Grandmother and George after helping George clear brush on a sultry summer afternoon when Grandmother mentioned that no one ever used the cabin and that we should check it out. Dad turned to me and asked, "Do you want to go to the lake sometime?" I eagerly jumped at the opportunity, and we started planning our first trip to the lake.

Dad and Grandmother

Late on the following Friday, Dad and I took off for the cabin, following the directions provided by George. The directions included several turns off of Highway 69, turning off the paved road, going past the large trailer park on the right, going right at the first Y in the road and left at the second Y, turning off the good gravel road onto the rough gravel road, and taking a right down a steep driveway that was barely visible just past the last rusted mailbox.

The sharp curves and steep hills were enough to scare anyone, or at least make them extremely car sick. I was skeptical and very queasy when we finally arrived at the cabin after dark.

The smell of mold and mildew nearly knocked me down the first time I stepped through the front door to the cabin into the kitchen that would have been outdated in the 1950's. As I walked through the kitchen, the floor creaked and gave slightly with each step, likely from some combination of rotting, termites, age, and neglect.

To the right of the kitchen was the "big" bedroom that was filled wall-to-wall by a queen mattress with no sheets or blankets. The dust exploded from the mattress with a soft pat.

A small bathroom with a toilet with rust colored water and a molded shower connected the big bedroom to the second bedroom, which was filled wall-to-wall by a twin mattress that was older and in worse shape than the queen mattress.

Outside of the second bedroom was a small living room with a hand-me-down couch that had seen better decades, a plywood coffee table, a chair with a broken spring, a glued piece of wood that held magazines, a closed off fireplace, and a faded and bubbled vinyl floor.

Outside the living room was a screened-in porch that was home to a variety of insects, arachnids, and rodents.

The cabin was nasty, full of spiders, a little dangerous, and likely could have been condemned for numerous reasons. Most people would have evacuated the cabin screaming. To me, it was magical and absolutely perfect.

It was completely dark outside when Dad and I finished walking through the cabin, unloaded our things, and sat down to eat a sandwich and a chocolate cruller from Piggly Wiggly. I ate as quickly as possible so that I could walk the seventy or so yards down to the water, which Dad told me was fine as long as I was careful.

After dinner, I stepped out of the front door, looked down to the water, and cautiously started the journey. My nerves were on edge as I slowly crept down the unfamiliar path to the lake.

After taking a few steps, I heard a flurry of noises that sounded like a combination of distressed rabid mountain lions, poisonous snakes, zombies, and other nightly terrors. Although it was likely nothing more than crickets, bullfrogs, and owls, I was terrified.

I cautiously continued down the path when, suddenly, I heard a crashing sound in the woods to the left. My young imagination exploded with possibilities, though the most likely scenario that I could come up with at the time was that the crazed, giant murderer hunting me in woods had tripped and knocked over a large pine tree. I then heard the unmistakable sound of steps in the woods to the left and nearly hyperventilated.

I froze on the path and tried to become one with a pine tree. My heart was in my throat when I saw a flash of tan along the wood line near the water, forty or so yards up to the left. As the large alpha-male beast materialized from the woods on the path in front of me, all I could do was stand completely still, try to squint so he couldn't see the white of my eyes, and hope that he didn't see me.

The beast was slowly walking across the path ahead of me when he stopped behind the two trees that framed the boathouse walkway just in front of the water. He turned slightly to his right and looked toward the cabin with what appeared to be dark, red eyes that pulsated with yellow flashes. He frantically scanned the area until his eyes fixed on his target, me.

Without logic or reason, I opened my eyes and looked into the beast's cold, dead eyes. Our gazes locked and we commenced a stare down, one which I would have happily lost if I hadn't been too terrified to blink, scream, or run.

The ravenous creature took two graceful steps to his right before he turned to face me. He was slowly stalking his prey, which was unfortunately going to be me.

The beast was between the two trees in front of the walkway to the boathouse when he squatted and made room for his next meal, which again was unfortunately going to be me. As soon as he finished, the crazed monster frantically charged me with the precision and speed of a mutant predator pursuing his prey and preparing to pounce. All I could muster the courage to do was stand there like an idiot with my mouth hanging toward the ground while trying not to cry.

As the beast ran toward me, I came to the realization that my time on earth was coming to an end and that I was about to meet my maker. I knew running wasn't an option – the beast would have caught me like a lion catches a gazelle in the African wilderness. I knew that climbing the tree wasn't an option – the beast would have either knocked the tree over or scaled it like a jaguar. My only options were to succumb to the wild animal or fight – and I wasn't willing to go down without a fight.

I channeled the fiercest warriors that I could think of at that age, the "wrasslers" of the WWF. As the beast approached, I crouched into the stance that typically follows the bell at the beginning of a match and prepared for the fight of my life – the fight *for* my life. My adrenalin increased with each step taken by the beast. I was a Real American with the Eye of the Tiger, and I was ready.

The beast, sensing the intensity and determination of his prey, stopped just short of me instead of pouncing. As he stopped, our eyes locked for the second time, and he hesitated. The tables were turning, and I had gained an advantage over the beast.

We were both frozen waiting for the other to make the first move when the beast broke the stalemate. I was not expecting his move and just stood there as he swiftly opened his mouth and launched at my right arm. I closed my eyes wincing in fear, the beast made contact, and I felt an unmistakable warmth cover my arm.

I quickly retracted and looked down to assess the damage and fend off the wild creature. Somehow, in those few seconds when my eyes had been closed, the ferocious beast had miraculously morphed into a friendly lab spending the weekend with his family at the lake, and he was frantically licking my arm and wagging his tail.

Realizing that my imagination had gotten away from me, I swallowed my heart, gave the beast a quick rub behind the ears, and then patted him as he took off toward a nearby cabin.

As the dog was running off, Dad stepped out of the cabin and asked me if everything was ok. I responded, "I'm fine – why don't you come with me?" As he walked out the door, he grabbed his yellow fiberglass spinning rod with a purple worm tied on and said that we would make a few casts from the dock.

Dad and I were walking together down the path toward the boathouse when I stopped him and said, "Don't walk between the trees." Dad looked at me like I was completely crazy and said in a confused tone, "What … why?" I nodded confidently and responded, "A dog just pooped between the trees – you don't want to step in it." Dad gave me a puzzled look as he walked around the tree shaking his head.

After we walked around the trees, I took several steps onto the boathouse walkway. For the first time, I was on the water at the Cove.

I closed my eyes, took a deep breath, and absorbed the cool breeze blowing from the spring that was behind the reeds at the back of the Cove. I delighted at the sounds of the outdoors that had scared me earlier that night. At that moment, and each of the thousands of times I stood in that same spot enjoying the outdoors after that night, I was completely relaxed and at peace.

I snapped out of the trance when Dad cleared his throat and repeated, "Buddy, do you want to cast?" I grabbed his old yellow spinning rod, squeezed the line with my right index finger, flipped the bail, and cast the purple worm to the dark waters.

As I was working the lure, Dad asked, "What do you think about the lake and the cabin?" I responded, "I love it, Dad." He smiled at me and said, "Me, too."

I reeled in the worm and made a second cast. The worm kissed the surface and the ripples faded into the night. I bounced the Texas-rigged worm a few times off the sandy bottom and felt an unmistakable thump, thump. I channeled the training I had received watching Bill Dance and Hank Parker on Saturday mornings as I reeled down, took a deep breath, and yanked the rod as hard as possible, nearly falling backward into the water. The ferocious hookset was clumsy, awkward, and anything but perfect. It was, however, good enough to hook the unsuspecting bass that bit Dad's purple worm.

After a short fight, I landed my first fish from the Cove, a skinny bass that was less than twelve inches long. I quickly unhooked the bass, said "Thank you buddy," and released it into the lake. As the fish swam away, Dad commented, "The lake seems to agree with you." I couldn't have agreed more.

After a few more casts, we called it a night, walked around the trees to dodge the beast's landmines, and headed up the path to spend our first night at the cabin.

After that night, we spent as much time as possible at the cabin. If we weren't at the cabin, I wanted to go. If someone ever mentioned the cabin, I took the opportunity to emphasize exactly how much I wanted to be there. I loved the cabin and every second I spent there.

Showing Grandmother how to make bass bigger in a photo!

The trip to the cabin became second nature, and the roads that had once petrified me became fun and exciting. I even learned how to drive on the dark and narrow roads to the cabin after I received my permit when I was fifteen. To this day, my heart flutters when I first catch a glimpse of the water while driving down Highway 69 toward lake Guntersville.

Paddle boating in my favorite lake

While staying at the cabin and fishing around the Cove, my love for fishing evolved into a passion. I truly cherished the time I spent fishing in and around the Cove, regardless of whether I was fishing from the dock outside of the boathouse, from the bank, from Grandmother's paddleboat, from George's green Jon boat or small fiberglass ski boat from the 1960's, from Dad's old Fisher aluminum bass boat that he bought from our neighbor, or from the Skeeter bass boat that I recently sold. I fished every season with every possible lure and loved every second.

It's easy ... see

While fishing around the Cove, I caught my biggest bass, the smallest bass imaginable, and countless fish in between. Every cast I made in the Cove was accompanied with hope, anticipation, and excitement. Every fish I landed, regardless of the size, was met with adrenalin and appreciation. Every time I missed or lost a fish, it was a giant, obviously. At the end of every trip, I was thankful for the experience and longed for the next trip.

Two at once on a Rat-L-Trap

At the time, I believed that my obsession with the Cove stemmed from a deep love of catching fish and a desire to catch as many fish as possible as often as possible. Looking back, I now realize that my love and obsession for the Cove was about much more than a rod, reel, and a fish on the end of the line.

Because of the time I spent fishing in the Cove, I can throw a baitcaster accurately, drive a boat, and occasionally find and catch fish. While I will always value these abilities, they pale in comparison to the memories of the Cove that are closest to my heart: cookouts with the family; watching the fog lift as the sun made its first appearance of the day over the mountains; learning that a boat can actually sink if you don't secure it correctly in a boathouse; finding common interests with Grandmother and developing a close relationship; swimming under the boathouse to retrieve the keys Dad left in the boat on a cold February afternoon, and then doing it again two weeks later; watching an escaped black panther walk along the shoreline and jumping at his bloodcurdling scream; watching grey bats blanket the sky at dusk; resting on the boat dock at night while listening to the sounds that had once terrified me; seeing the smiles on the faces of friends and family as they caught their first or biggest fish; and always avoiding the path between the two trees next to the boathouse walkway. These experiences and memories helped shape who I am today, and they are far more important than any bass I could have ever caught in the Cove.

Enjoying the Cove with Sunni and Dad

Shortly following Grandmother's death, the cabin was sold. While I would have loved to buy the cabin, it wasn't possible for a poor student.

A few days before the closing, I spent one last afternoon alone at the cabin. Emotions flooded over me when I walked out the front door for the last time and looked back at the cabin with wonder. The cabin was truly a magical place, and the Cove will always be part of who I am.

I will always treasure the Cove.

7
Not Anymore

Jake is my oldest friend. He and I have been like brothers since we were born. Our parents have been friends forever and were in each other's weddings, our sisters have been friends forever and were in each other's weddings, and, of course, Jake and I were in each other's weddings.

Before Jake joined the Marines, he and I frequently hunted together on the Wheeler Wildlife Refuge, or "the Refuge" as we always called it. In fact, he showed me several of my all-time favorite spots on the Refuge.

Many Saturday mornings during bow season, Jake and I would meet early in the morning and either jump in his Bronco or my Blazer and head to the Refuge to hunt. We had many memorable trips, but one particular trip on a Saturday in November will always stand out.

Jake played high school football on Friday nights. After games, our options for entertainment in a small town in North Alabama were generally very limited. While the local McDonalds parking lot was always an option, the preferable choice was a "pasture party" in a nearby cow pasture.

Pasture parties took on many different forms, but generally involved cars parked along the edge of a woodline, large bon fires, the occasional beer, and a lot of stupidity. Except for the rare time when someone was convinced that "cow tipping" was a real thing, the cows were generally safe (at least the four-legged kind).

On this particular Friday night, the football game was rough, and our Tigers lost. A few of Jake's teammates were going to a party after the game and asked him to go. He asked me to join, but I declined, opting to go home and get some rest before the morning hunt.

Jake went out that night, had a great time, and may have had a few too many. After the party, his friends dropped him off at his house. He snuck in the front door without waking up his dad in the recliner and crept down the hall to get a few hours of much needed sleep.

Jake was supposed to meet Ben and me at my house the next morning around 3:30 AM. Ben and I were outside waiting when Jake finally pulled into the driveway about thirty minutes late. Jake was generally very prompt, so I suspected that something wasn't quite right. My suspicions were confirmed when he opened the car door and fell out of his Bronco into the driveway. He was obviously struggling. My dog Casper, who always loved Jake, didn't even go to him that morning.

When I saw Jake, I laughed and said, "Rough night, huh, – why don't you go get in the bed instead of going hunting?" He was adamant that we were going hunting.

We loaded his old Summit stand and his bow into the Blazer and took off to one of our favorite spots on the Refuge near the Tennessee River.

We parked next to a gate down a small embankment alongside a busy road on that cool November morning. We were all wearing camo and Jake had his old trusted black toboggan.

When I turned on the light in the Blazer, I saw that Jake was as green as his camo. I asked, "Are you going to be OK?" Jake responded with a deep and urgent grunt as he threw open the door and ran to the woods about twenty feet away.

Jake proceeded to lose everything he had eaten and drunk the night before on the edge of the woods as Ben and I sat there and laughed at him. About that time, we saw blue lights – on the road, and panicked.

A police unit was stopped by the road and two state troopers were getting out of the car. Ben and I rushed up the embankment to meet them, in order to keep everyone as far away from Jake as possible.

The first trooper looked at us suspiciously and said, "What are you boys doing out this time of the night?" We tried to hide our cracking, scared voices when we responded, "We are high school students and came here to bow hunt on the Refuge."

The second trooper, who by this time had joined us, commented, "It looks like it will be a good day for hunting – you boys be careful." Ben and I both said, "Thank you, Sir" at the same time and took off back down the embankment.

Ben and I felt like outlaws as we strutted confidently back to the Blazer. As we took a step off the hill, we saw that Jake was also hobbling back.

The three of us met back at the Blazer about the same time. As soon as we arrived, the first trooper, who apparently wasn't satisfied with our discussion, yelled, "You boys got any alcohol?" Before Ben and I could answer, Jake yelled, "NOT ANYMORE!"

Ben and I were mortified. We had no idea what to say or do, and we were both certain that we were going to prison. Jake, however, was smiling from ear-to-ear. The trooper laughed, shook his head, wished us luck, and went on his way.

I'm not sure how long Ben and I stood there staring at where the trooper had been parked, but the next thing I remember is Jake, who by this time had his stand on his back and his bow in his hand, urging Ben and me to hurry.

Ben and I grabbed our stands and bows and, shortly before 5:00 that morning, all three of us set off through the field towards our destinations in the woods. As we walked to the woods, we agreed to meet at the edge of the field at 9:30 to head home.

After the morning hunt, Ben and I met on the edge of the field right at 9:30 as planned. Jake, however, was late again. After a few minutes, I became worried and decided to go look for him.

I knew where Jake was climbing, so I told Ben to stay in the field while I went to check on him. I walked down a large trail where we often found deer droppings toward where Jake was supposed to climb.

The woods were completely silent, and I became increasingly worried about Jake with each step that I took. When I turned the corner, I urgently looked up Jake's tree and saw something that I had never seen and hope to never see again. There, twenty feet up in a tree was Jake, or rather Jake's pale white rear, hanging off the edge of his tree stand.

Jake had tightened his safety belt so he could stand on the edge of his treestand while facing the tree in a full squat.

I yelled at Jake with a combination of shock and disgust, and all he said was, "I had to go, Man – I'll be out in a little while." Traumatized, I walked back to the field to meet up with Ben and to tell him what had happened.

Ben thought it was hilarious, which was easy for him since he wasn't the one near the drop zone.

A few minutes later, Jake walked into the field laughing. Ben and Jake had a good laugh at my misfortune. Frustrated and nauseated, I asked Jake, "Why didn't you wait instead of ruining the spot." Jake responded, "When you've got to go, you've got to go."

As we were walking back to the Blazer, I noticed that Jake wasn't wearing his favorite black toboggan. In a confused tone, I asked, "Do you have your toboggan?" Jake responded matter-of-factly, "Not anymore." I knew from his answer that it was best to leave it alone.

Jake joined the Marines before the next hunting season. Ben and I were still seniors in high school at the time and were planning to hunt the same area. A few weeks before bow season, Ben and I were scouting the same trail where Jake had climbed the previous year reminiscing about that day with Jake.

When we reached Jake's tree, I was looking at the ground for deer droppings when I noticed something black just beside my foot. For the second time next to Jake's tree in less than a year, I was traumatized and mortified. There, beside my foot, was Jake's soiled signature black toboggan, exactly where he had dropped it the year before.

I didn't know whether to laugh, cry, or vomit. I did know that I needed to get out of there as quickly as possible.

After the second incident standing underneath Jake's tree in less than one year, Jake's tree was officially retired. Ben and I frequently hunted the Refuge after that day, but neither of us ever went back to Jake's tree.

Both Ben and Jake were groomsmen at my wedding a decade or so later. I decided that I wanted to do something unique, special and memorable for each groomsman. I thought Jake, who has always been one of the calmest and most collected persons I've ever known, was going to lose it when I handed him a new black toboggan in front of the entire wedding party and told him it was to replace the one he had lost on the Refuge. Red faced and embarrassed, all he could do was shrug his shoulders and give me a hug.

8
Patches

Before choosing which college to attend, I made a list of the factors that were most important to me: nearby places to hunt, outstanding fishing opportunities, and close proximity to a beach. I also wanted to stay in Alabama, if possible.

Given my priorities, I decided that the best option was the University of South Alabama in Mobile, better known as USA. After choosing USA, I verified that majoring in Computer Science was an option, since I had picked that major in the seventh grade and was too stubborn to reconsider.

Saying goodbye to Casper and off to college

When I arrived in Mobile, I immediately realized that I made a mistake – hunting and fishing gear wasn't allowed in the dorm. Also, proximity to the beach really shouldn't be a top priority in choosing a school (especially when it was still a hair over 106 minute round trip to the beach, approximately).

About a month into the fall semester at USA, I had an overwhelming urge to go shooting or hunting. Since I didn't have guns or hunting gear and couldn't afford new gear (and wouldn't have anywhere to store it even if I could have afforded it), I needed a new plan.

Late one afternoon, I had an idea that was flawless and epic, or at least I thought. I went to a local sporting goods store and purchased a slingshot with a fold back wrist brace for stability, duct tape that was Realtree camouflage, steel balls, and targets. I immediately went back to the dorm, used the duct tape to make the slingshot camouflage, and set targets in the woods outside of the dorm window for practice. My roommate Matt thought I was nuts, but he was happy to participate once he realized I couldn't be dissuaded.

I became a crack shot with the slingshot within a few days and was quickly becoming famous in the dorm for my shooting skills. Several of the guys in the dorm, including the resident advisor, Tee, frequently stopped by the dorm room to shoot the slingshot and challenge me to a shooting competition.

Tee had warned me that the slingshot violated the rules of the dorm. However, he agreed to let me keep it as long I was careful, if no one in administration caught me, and I let him shoot with me. Of course I agreed.

A week or so later, I was hanging out the window shooting targets with Matt just before dark. I was in the process of grabbing a steel ball when Matt gasped. I looked at him puzzled and said,

"What's wrong?" He pointed frantically in the woods and exclaimed, "There is a wild animal out there."

Without thinking or hesitating, I grabbed the slingshot and jumped through the window of our first floor dorm room in order to protect the unknowing students in the dorm from whatever wild creature was roaming the woods. After crashing to the ground, I scanned the area to assess the situation. About that time, I saw a flash beside a tree, and a massive raccoon stepped out.

The raccoon was just slightly smaller than a Great Dane and was not afraid of me in the least. In fact, it acted like it was going to come after me. I was convinced the gigantic raccoon was rabid and would attack me and everyone else in the dorm. As soon as it took the first step toward me, instincts took over and I let a steel ball fly from the slingshot with the focus and confidence of Robin Hood on Ritalin.

I had no doubt that, given my extensive practice and preparation, the shot would hit the mark. It was as if time slowed to a crawl when I released the steel ball. It took what seemed like an eternity for the steel ball to fly through the air toward the raccoon, which was standing on the edge of the woods just outside of the dorm window.

I hit the fierce raccoon in the head, and he dropped like a rock. I had done it – I had slayed the beast and protected all of the residents in the dorm from the rabid, wild predator.

After the shot, Matt was cheering and screaming loudly. I felt like I had saved the world while watching Rocky. I thought I was a hero.

I was preparing to jump back in the window when Matt took off to our door. As I struggled to climb back in the window, Tee walked in to check on the commotion and take a few shots with the slingshot.

As Tee was walking through the room, Matt cheered, "Corey just got a raccoon with his slingshot!" and held his hand up to give Tee five. I suspected something wasn't quite right when Tee, who was standing there with his mouth open, didn't share Matt's joy or give him five. My suspicions were confirmed when Tee looked up at me with a shocked look on his face and a tear in his eye and said in a broken voice, "You ... killed ... Patches."

I was speechless and mortified as Tee emotionally explained that Patches was a regular at the dorm and that a group of people had been feeding him out of their windows. I felt horrible.

Before I could apologize to Tee, Matt chimed in and said, "Don't worry, Corey made a great shot and Patches didn't suffer." I shook my head and whispered under my voice in a sarcastic tone, "Thanks, Matt – that really helped." Tee turned and stormed out of our room.

That night, I became known as the "guy that shot Patches." I apologized profusely to anyone that I hurt or offended. I still regret and feel bad for shooting Patches.

The following morning, I jumped out of the window and walked to the spot where Patches had fallen the night before. I felt terrible for shooting Patches and planned to give him a proper burial. I searched everywhere, but, to my surprise, Patches was nowhere to be found. I like to think that Patches walked off during the night with little more than a headache.

I retired the trusted slingshot the evening I shot Patches, and I haven't shot it since. The slingshot wasn't as good an idea as I had thought. The incident with Patches also confirmed that USA wasn't a good fit for me and that it was probably a good idea to transfer to another school, preferably one that offered better hunting and fishing opportunities.

The real archer when he goes afield enters a land of subtle delight. The dew glistens on the leaves, the thrush sings in the bush, the soft wind blows, and all nature welcomes him as she has the hunter since the world began. With the bow in his hand, his arrows softly rustling in the quiver, a horn at his back, and a hound at his heels, what more can a man want in life?

Saxton Pope

I reckon if I want Frazier to fix this door, I'm gonna have to dangle a minner in front of it.

Gladys Louise Elliott Sulcer – "Sussie"

9

The Hangup

It doesn't matter the day, the weather, or the conditions, Dad believes that any fish within 100 yards of a six-inch purple curly tail worm, a quarter ounce chrome and blue Rat-L-Trap, or a 1980's baby bass Bomber crankbait will always bite. Dad's list of secret lures didn't include an old Bomber crankbait until a fall day in the mid 1990's.

It was a chilly autumn afternoon. Dad and I had fished worms for several hours along a rock wall that we frequently fished on the lower end of Guntersville in a fourteen-foot green aluminum Jon boat with a fifteen-horsepower Johnson motor. We had caught and released a few small fish, but it was obvious to Dad that there were no big fish within 100 yards to bite his purple worm.

As dusk was approaching, Dad proclaimed, "Last cast." We both made one final cast, worked our worms to the boat, and called it a day.

As we were packing up, Dad commented, "Let's tie on Rat-L-Traps and troll back to the dock." Unfortunately for Dad, the only chrome and blue Rat-L-Trap in the boat was tied to the spinning rod that he and Mom had just given me for my birthday. After scavenging his double sided Plano tackle box, Dad reluctantly tied on an old Bomber 6A crankbait in a baby bass color that was discontinued in the 1980's. We both threw the lures behind the boat as Dad twisted the throttle on the old Johnson motor.

On the ride back to the cabin, we were discussing where we would fish the next day and what we hoped to catch. Neither of us was paying much attention when Dad had to quickly grab his rod to keep it from flying into the water.

Dad frantically shut off the motor and was thankfully able to save his favorite rod and reel, a five and a half foot Fenwick casting rod with an Abu Garcia 5500C baitcaster that Mom had bought for him for Fathers' Day a few years earlier. Dad yanked his rod fiercely and repetitively and seethed, "I'm stuck on a log." Just as he was about to give up, he pointed behind the boat and commented, "Look over there – the log is coming to the boat."

Dad and I were watching the log come across the surface when the log suddenly shook its head and soared through the air. Dad's calm and collected demeanor vanished as he screamed, "It's not a log, it's a huge hawg!" Dad stood up in the old Jon boat and fought the fish all the way to the boat, somehow avoiding dumping us in the cool October waters. I put the net under the giant bass as soon as it was alongside the boat.

We were both speechless when I swung the fish into the boat. Dad had fished his entire life without catching a bass over six pounds. On that October afternoon, Dad had landed the largest bass of his life, a largemouth that weighed right at seven and a half pounds, using an old Bomber crankbait that he was only throwing because we were out of Rat-L-Traps and then after trying to shake the fish off thinking it was a log.

Dad's confidence in the baby bass Bomber crankbait increased throughout the fall as he landed countless bass on the lure.

Dad's big bass on an ancient Bomber 6A

A month or so after he caught his first seven-pounder, we were once again trolling down the same pass. Dad was using his secret baby bass Bomber crankbait waiting for another monster to attack his lure, and I was sitting in the front of the Jon boat lost in my thoughts and enjoying the outdoors.

I was brought back to reality when the boat violently rocked while Dad grunted, cursed, and complained, "I'm stuck on a log." We both watched with excitement and anticipation as Dad stood in the boat and vigorously shook his rod. Unfortunately, his lure was actually hung this time.

Dad's frustration was overwhelming as he frantically shook his rod trying to save his secret lure. Realizing that his tactic wasn't working, Dad adopted a new strategy. He stood on the tips of his toes, leaned back deeply, and bowed his rod in hopes of pulling his beloved lure free.

When his rod was bowed to the max, Dad's line finally went slack. Unfortunately, the slack line occurred simultaneously with a snapping sound very similar to a .22 rifle. Dad's only baby bass Bomber crankbait from the 1980's was gone forever.

To make the situation even worse, when his line snapped, Dad lost his balance and tumbled backward into the frigid lake. His fall was anything but graceful, and the deep splash was accompanied by the loud pop of his favorite Fenwick rod snapping. He had lost his only baby bass Bomber crankbait, broken his favorite rod, and taken a swim in the November waters of Guntersville in a matter of seconds. It was a bad day.

I helped Dad back in the boat and we headed to the dock in complete silence so he could walk up to the cabin to dry off. A few minutes later, I was standing on the back porch when I heard Dad walk up behind me. I turned and said, "I'm really sorry you lost your baby bass crankbait Dad." In a sorrowful tone, Dad responded, "Me too, but its ok – we'll find another one."

For many years after he lost his favorite crankbait, we looked everywhere for a replacement baby bass Bomber crankbait from the 1980's. We finally decided that either they don't exist or no one would ever be crazy enough to lose or get rid of one. After all, they will catch any bass within 100 yards.

A few years ago, I asked Dad to go smallmouth fishing with me. It wasn't easy to talk him into fishing with new lures, but he reluctantly agreed after a lot of convincing.

By early afternoon, Dad had not caught a single fish and was beginning to question his decision to fish with the new lures. He was clearly frustrated when he exclaimed, "What am I doing wrong?" I looked back at Dad and asked, "How many times have you been hung up today?" He gave me a confused look and said, "None – why?" I then explained that his lure needed to be in the rocks to catch big smallmouth, which would necessarily mean hang-ups and breakoffs.

On his next cast, I overheard Dad mumbling in the back of the boat that he was hung. He was shaking his rod violently trying to free his lure as I walked to the back of the boat to help him. I was explaining that being hung was a good thing when I noticed that his line was taking off to the surface and yelled, "Dad – You've got a fish." I thought he was going to fall out of the boat when the monster smallmouth at the end of his line broke the surface. The log that he thought he was hung on was a huge trophy smallmouth.

The fight was long and tiresome, for Dad, the fish, and me. I netted his gargantuan fish as soon as she surfaced by the boat. I will never forget the look on Dad's face when he grabbed the smallmouth of a lifetime, a seven-pound two-ounce behemoth. It was the first seven-pound bass he had caught since losing his old baby bass Bomber crankbait a few decades earlier.

We released the smallmouth to swim another day after weighing her and taking pictures. As we watched her swim away, I noticed that Dad was shaking his head and laughing. Puzzled, I asked, "What's wrong Dad." All he could say was how glad he was that he hadn't been hung on a log or shaken the fish off his hook.

Dad with the smallmouth bass of a lifetime.

10
The Grill and the Road

Ben and I first met when we were six. I was tall with a giant head, and he had enormous front teeth and looked like a beaver. At the time, we both aspired to be professional athletes, at least some days.

Our dads coached us at sports starting at a very young age. Somewhere along the way, they devised a scheme to co-coach a little league basketball team, the Pistons. By co-coaching, they exploited the league rules requiring a son to play for his father and ensured that Ben and I both played for the Pistons. In their words, they were creating "a little league powerhouse super-team." We won the league championship several years until the league changed the rules.

During the years we played for the Pistons, Ben and I became inseparable. As we got older, we eventually shifted from basketball and other sports to hunting and fishing. Together, we have logged countless hours in the woods and on the water.

During the summer after our freshman year in college, Ben and I saw each other regularly and spoke daily. By the middle of the summer, our focus revolved primarily around deer hunting the following fall.

After numerous discussions, we agreed that it was time to find somewhere to hunt other than the Wheeler Wildlife Refuge. We both truly loved the Refuge, but we were convinced that we needed to find better hunting land with more and bigger deer.

We started our search for a perfect hunting camp that would be close to one of our schools, the University of Alabama or the University of Alabama at Birmingham. The land also needed to provide ample opportunities for giant bucks. We feared that it would be difficult to find that ideal hunting camp that had giant bucks and that was a short drive from Tuscaloosa and Birmingham, but we were ready for the challenge.

Shortly after we started our search, we found our first lead. A cousin mentioned that when he stopped at a gas station in Cullman, he saw an advertisement for a hunting club in Northport. We were excited about the possibility, since Northport was just outside of Tuscaloosa. We immediately started our quest to find the gas station and the hunting club in Northport.

A few days later, we pulled into the gas station, found the advertisement for the club, called the number on the ad, and spoke with the president. After a very short call, we heard everything that we needed to hear (mainly that there were allegedly "giants" on the property). Without setting foot on the land or talking to any of the members, we agreed on the spot to join the club and pay the dues, which wasn't easy for two hungry college students.

We weren't worried that the club had several thousand acres or nearly fifty members. We figured that the skills we had developed hunting the Refuge equipped us to easily learn the land and find the monster bucks promised by the club president. We had no doubt that we would find that perfect spot and, come fall, we would be decorating our walls with trophy antlers with long and thick tines and have venison to spare.

A few weeks after joining the club and getting our gate keys, we decided to take a trip for the weekend to scout, learn the land, hunt wild boar, and camp. Unfortunately, all of our hunting and camping gear was still at our parents' houses.

In order for us to spend the weekend at Northport, Ben drove an hour from Tuscaloosa to pick me up from my apartment in Birmingham. We then drove an hour and a half further north to our parents' houses to fill his Toyota 4Runner with our camping and hunting gear. When we finished packing Ben's car, you could not see out the back window.

Before we headed out on the three hour journey south to the hunting club, we stopped by his aunt's house to "borrow" the most beautiful, thick ribeye steaks from the freezer in her garage. We even grabbed sea salt, red pepper, and Cavender's seasoning. We could already see and smell those perfectly seasoned ribeyes sizzling underneath the stars, and they sure looked and smelled delicious. We were two woodsmen on a mission, and we had enough gear to survive a zombie apocalypse.

We finally arrived at the hunting camp in Northport a few hours after lunch. We decided to spend the afternoon driving every gravel road on the property to learn the land and get our bearings. The plan was to spend the next morning on foot to scout promising areas and maybe come across an unsuspecting wild boar to hunt, since boar season was the only hunting season open that time of the year.

After driving all afternoon and evening on the old dusty roads around the property, we started making our way back to camp for our steak dinner under the stars.

We made it back a few minutes before dusk and shared a few evening refreshments as we unloaded the 4Runner and started setting up camp. We pulled out the tent, the coolers, sleeping bags, pillows, a hatchet, a machete, guns, bows, and everything else we had packed for the trip. When we pulled out the last bag from the back of Ben's 4Runner, I turned to him and asked, "Where'd you put the grill?" He snidely retorted, "You were supposed to get the grill, not me." After several minutes of finger pointing and heated arguing, we agreed to disagree. To this day, we blame each other for forgetting the grill.

Regardless of whose fault it was, we had a major problem. We were stranded in Northport since neither of us was willing to drive the miles of narrow gravel roads back to Tuscaloosa at night, especially after sharing a few beverages. We also had no way to cook our steaks. Not knowing what else to do, we made a fire and started discussing options and our next steps.

A few drinks later, we came to the realization that we were no closer to our dreams of perfectly seasoned medium-rare steaks under the stars. Our ideas were progressively getting worse. We were hungry and frustrated and about ready to kill each other.

Neither of us had spoken a word for some time when Ben slapped his knee, stood up, and said, "Why don't we walk around and see if we can find something to use as a grill." Not having any better ideas, I reluctantly agreed. We put a few spare drinks in our pockets and took off on foot, at night, and with nothing but a hatchet and Ben's trusted pistol to find something that we could use to grill the steaks.

After walking throughout the main camp area, we came across a handmade shed from the early 1900's that had succumbed to age and the elements. The only thing we found in the shed ruins was termites, spiders, roaches, and wasps. However, the shed did have an old rusted tin roof.

One of us had the brilliant idea to cut off a piece from the grey and brown tin roof, put the piece of rusted tin on the fire to heat it and hopefully kill the bacteria, then sear the steaks on it. We agreed that the tin was the solution to our missing grill problem and started putting our plan into action.

After cutting a few feet of tin roof with the old hatchet and dragging it back to the fire, we were in business. We made a small table with logs, propped the piece of tin a few inches above the fire, and watched the smoke billowing off the tin as the fire heated the surface and burned off decades of dirt, rust, and corrosion.

It was right at midnight before we agreed that the tin was hot enough to sear the steaks. By this time, we were starving and had drunk several more than we intended. As we were preparing to toss the steaks on the makeshift grill, we doused the hot tin with beer and dumped all of our red pepper through the steam from the sizzling beer to sanitize the tin and give the steaks an incredible flavor. We then tossed the steaks on the tin in the middle of the sizzling red pepper.

After searing the steaks for three to four minutes on each side, we removed them from our red-hot tin grill. Moments later, we were enjoying every juicy morsel of our red pepper encrusted ribeyes.

We were finally living our dreams of ribeye steaks under the stars. Both of our recollections are fuzzy on how the steaks actually tasted, but we both said at the time that the beer and red pepper gave them a great flavor and that the steaks were the best ever, even though they were seared on an old, rusted, and dirty tin roof that we cut off a rotten shed with a hatchet.

It was after one in the morning when we finally finished dinner. As soon as we took the last bite, we each realized that the other had forgotten to set up the tent. Too tired to argue, we decided to leave the tent in the bag and sleep in Ben's 4Runner, with him in the driver's seat and me in the passenger's seat. It wasn't the first time we had slept in his 4Runner, and it definitely wouldn't be the last.

We were awakened by the sun what felt like a few minutes later. We felt terrible from the beer and the tin-seared red pepper ribeyes from the night before, but neither of us would admit it. After all, we were woodsmen from Alabama, and we were on a mission.

We drove to a secluded part of the hunting land, parked, and set out on foot with our trusted weapons, stomach aches, and hangovers. After walking for what seemed like hours looking for either the perfect place to deer hunt in the upcoming fall season or for an unsuspecting wild boar, we finally came across an oak bottom near a creek that would be incredible for bow hunting in October when the acorns dropped.

After a few minutes, our excitement about the oak bottom waned as we propped against two small trees, held our stomachs, and tried to cool off and hopefully feel better. I was sweating profusely and struggling to keep my head up when I groaned, "Man, I don't feel good." Ben was obviously struggling as he whined, "Me, neither, I'm gonna be sick."

We had a difficult decision to make. We were in a spot that we wanted to hunt, and neither of us wanted to ruin it. At the same time, we both felt terrible and were going to be sick. Not willing to abandon any hope of hunting the oak bottom, we decided to get out of there immediately.

We had seen another trail that went up a hill when we first walked into the oak bottom. After frantically discussing our options, we decided to take the trail and hopefully find a suitable bathroom in the woods, preferably in a secluded area with a nice breeze.

We waddled up the trail and finally reached a clearing. We made the snap decision that I would go left along the edge of the clearing and the woodline and Ben would go right. We were far enough apart that we could just barely see each other's heads while we were doing our business and deeply regretting our decisions from the night before.

Shortly after we settled at the latrines in the woods, we both yanked our heads to the left at a humming sound that was getting progressively louder. Confused and a little worried, I hollered to Ben, "What's that noise." Ben shrugged his shoulders and shouted back, "No clue, but it's getting closer."

Moments later, we were shocked, mortified, and embarrassed when we learned that the source of the humming was an old grey Honda driving less than four feet in front of us on the main road that we had mistaken as a clearing. The man and the woman in the car were obviously shocked and offended to see two red-faced, sweaty guys in full camo squatting next to the main road. Not knowing what else to do, we both waved.

We had unknowingly circled back to the main road that was just outside of the gate to the hunting club. We had not realized our miscalculation in the frantic rush to find a safe and secluded location to deal with our regrettable decisions from the previous night.

A few minutes later, Ben and I met on the road in the clearing. Ben looked at me and said, "You wanna just walk on the road back to the truck." I simply nodded. Ben laughed and said, "You don't want to talk about what just happened, do you?" I closed my eyes, shook my head, and said the only word that seemed appropriate at the time, "Nope!"

After a short walk down the paved road, we jumped the gate into the hunting club and walked a few hundred yards to Ben's 4Runner. We then drove back to camp in silence. We quickly loaded up the car and left the hunting camp in Northport.

As we drove away, I turned to Ben and said, "You know, the Refuge really isn't that bad." Ben nodded his head and said, "You're telling me."

Ben and I never went back to the hunting camp in Northport. We decided that the club wasn't a good fit for us after all – that or we didn't want to run into the people from the grey Honda.

11
The Fishing Nut

When I decided to go to law school, I was confident in the decision. I had no doubts or hesitation. During orientation, my thoughts and feelings shifted exclusively to doubt and hesitation and generally stayed there. In fact, I was convinced I had made a big mistake and questioned whether I should even show up for the first day.

As I drove to law school on the first day of classes, I stopped at a red light at a four-way intersection. I wrestled with whether to take a left to go to the law school, to go straight and head to the beach, or to go right and head to the lake.

While I sat there weighing the options, the light must have changed without me noticing. I was startled when the guy in the Chevy truck behind me honked and showed me his favorite finger. I quickly floored it and went left without thinking, to the law school.

Later that morning in my first class, the professor, who had just moved to the South from Massachusetts, went around the room and asked each person to state his or her name and provide a little background information. Almost everyone in the class talked about their dream to be an attorney or why they wanted to be an attorney.

When the professor finally looked at me, all I could think to say was, "My name is Corey – I have a degree in Computer Science and I really like to hunt and fish." The professor's eyes widened and her face distorted as she scowled in disgust. It was obvious that the professor had never spent any time in the outdoors as she looked at me like I was a crazed murderer with no business being in law school. I decided at that moment that I should have taken a right that morning and gone fishing.

A few minutes later, someone on the other side of the class spoke up and said, "My name is Drew and I'm nuts about fishing." I realized then that there was hope, and I immediately knew that Drew and I were going to be friends. After class, Drew and I met in the hall and started talking about fishing.

Drew went to college at Wake Forest and had fished his entire life, mostly in the mountains and in Southern Alabama along the Gulf Coast. He had spent very little time bass fishing, but was interested in trying it. He mentioned that he really hoped he could fish Lake Guntersville sometime. I told him that I fished Guntersville all the time and described the small cabin at the back of a slough on the lower end of Guntersville, or the "Cove" as we always called it. We immediately started planning a trip.

Drew and I decided to plan our trip for early October when the bass generally school up and feed before winter. Crankbait fishing on Guntersville in the fall was an annual tradition for Dad and me, and one of my favorite things. After telling Drew about past autumn trips, we were both excited and ready to go.

The week leading up to our trip, Drew asked me what we would be fishing with and what he needed to bring. I told him to bring a few baitcasters with twelve to fifteen-pound test line, a few spinning rods with eight- to ten- pound test line, natural colored zoom flukes from three to five inches, 3/0 Gamagatsu offset hooks, a few Bill Lewis chrome and blue Rat-L-Traps with each back hook swapped out to a number two black Xcalibur treble hook, and a few six to ten foot diving crankbaits in either shad or baby bass colors. Drew looked at me like I was speaking an unknown foreign language in a Southern accent. I'm not sure how much he understood of what I said, but I don't think it was much. I finally told Drew just to bring his favorite rods and that I would provide the rest.

Since Drew had very little experience with a baitcasting reel, he opted for his light saltwater spinning rod. After discussing lures, Drew decided on the Rat-L-Trap. Once we rigged up, I drove the boat downriver to fish a slough where I had found fish the previous year on a five to six foot flat with a few stumps next to a steep drop off.

After twenty or thirty minutes, we weren't having any luck. I told Drew not to worry and that the fish would often start schooling and busting out of the water chasing baitfish as if a switch had been flipped.

Drew was cautiously optimistic as he prepared for a cast I will never forget. He held the line on his rod with his index finger as he flipped the bail, reared back, swung his rod forward, and released the lure. His line peeled off his spinning reel and made a small rainbow as it floated toward the water where his Rat-L-Trap gently kissed the surface. The cast was picture perfect – it could not have been better.

His line spanned the edge of the ridge where the flat transitioned to deep water, likely in front of a hungry bass. It was one of those casts where you just knew he would catch something.

As soon as I reeled in my lure, I decided to take a break, watch him bring in the Rat-L-Trap, and hopefully see him set the hook on a monster. I remember looking up at the sky and deeply enjoying the crisp October afternoon, the green waters of Guntersville, and the surrounding mountains with trees showing a hint of fall color.

Drew was working the lure like a pro, and I was eagerly awaiting the hook set. When his lure was a few feet from the boat, Drew felt a massive strike and, using every ounce of strength he had, set the hook fiercely. It was a hookset that would have made Bill Dance proud. Drew was finally fishing Guntersville, and I was watching him closely to see how he handled the giant.

About the time Drew set the hook, what felt like an angry prehistoric bug bit me on my right jaw between my eye and my ear. I slapped my cheek aggressively to kill the bug and then tried to throw it off of my jaw. Unfortunately, the bug didn't move. In fact, the culprit was not a bug – it was a Bill Lewis quarter ounce chrome and blue Rat-L-Trap with a number two Xcalibur treble hook that was attached to Drew's line. It was now attached TO me!

I came to the quick and unfortunate realization that the hook was buried deep in my jaw well past the barb. I don't remember exactly what I yelled at that moment, and that is probably a good thing.

Xcalibur hooks are curved slightly to dig deeper when pulled to ensure a solid hookset. These hooks work flawlessly, and each time I tried to wiggle the hook out, it dug deeper into my jaw. There was no pulling the hook out. The first thing that Drew caught on Guntersville was me, and he had caught me good.

We both quickly realized that our trip was coming to an untimely end, and that I needed to go to the hospital. I cut the line to the Drew's lure, sat down, fired up the Mercury outboard, and took off back to the Cove with one hand holding the Rat-L-Trap in my face and one hand on the wheel.

As I turned the boat by the rock wall leading into the Cove, it was like a switch flipped and fish started busting everywhere. It looked like the water in the Cove was boiling. There were what seemed like thousands of bass and stripe coming out of the water in the Cove chasing baitfish. I had never seen anything like it. It was an opportunity of a lifetime for a fisherman, and we were about to miss it to get Drew's Rat-L-Trap surgically removed from my face.

When we were pulling up to the dock, Drew's head was down and he looked miserable because of what happened. He looked over at me and said in a sad voice, "I'm really sorry – is this gonna be the last time we fish together?" I told him it was an accident, that I had been fishing my entire life without being hooked in the face, and that something like that was a one-in-a-million situation and would never happen again.

I then looked sternly at Drew and said as seriously as I could muster, "Besides, I think the Rat-L-Trap in the face is a good look for me – I may keep it." Drew was relieved by my joke, and we both jumped out of the boat and headed back to the cabin.

Dad met us at the front door as we walked up the path to the cabin. As soon as he saw the Rat-L-Trap in my face, he confirmed that we needed to go to the hospital. As we were getting ready to leave, I couldn't stop thinking about the fish. We were about to walk out the door when I abruptly stopped Dad and Drew and told them to get me a piece of ice and wire cutters, and for both of them to leave the cabin and sit on the porch.

They both realized what I was planning at the same time. Dad wasn't really that surprised. After all, he raised me and would have done the same thing to catch fish. Drew, on the other hand, looked like he was going to vomit. He was pale white and kept asking if I was serious as if I was playing a practical joke on him. I finally convinced both Dad and Drew to leave me.

In my mind, the plan was simple and easy: I would numb the area around the hook with the ice, the hook point would easily puncture the skin without any hesitation or pain, I would cut off the barb and slide the hook back out of the two holes in my face, I would take two ibuprofens, and I would be catching fish within the hour as if nothing had happened. I was wrong. I was very wrong.

I tried to hold the ice beside the hook without a towel. I ended up with a wet face and numb fingers, which made a tough situation even more difficult. It was about that time when I finally questioned the decision to rip a hook through my jaw as part of an elaborate plan to maybe catch a few fish. For the first time since I had my brilliant idea to save the fishing trip, I was ready to go to the hospital. I walked out of the bathroom to tell Dad and Drew that we were going to the hospital.

As I stepped in the kitchen, I gazed to the lake. The water around the boathouse was visible from the kitchen, and I swear a dozen bass jumped at the exact moment I looked out the window, each one taunting me. The urge to fish overwhelmed me. I wanted those fish. I needed those fish.

Without thinking or hesitating, I grabbed the hook, violently pressed the tip of the hook as hard as I could until it ripped through the other side of my jaw past the barb, and proceeded to scream louder than I had ever screamed in my life.

With tears in my eyes and blood dripping down my face, I did my best to hold the hook in place with my shaky hands. I then stumbled to the bathroom, cut the barb of the hook off with the wire cutters, yanked what was left of the treble hook out of the two holes in my face left by the the hook, and poured peroxide on the holes.

I walked out of the bathroom with blood and peroxide dripping down my face and met Dad and Drew on the porch. Before either could speak, I held up my right hand to quiet them and proclaimed sternly, "I am going fishing now." Drew was shocked and a little queasy from the blood when he exclaimed in the most serious tone I had ever heard, "You are a man!" It was an awkward moment, but not one that would keep me from the fish.

Drew and I fished in the Cove that afternoon and had an incredible day. If memory serves me correctly, we caught fifty-three fish, including numerous bass between three and six pounds (all of which were released to swim and be caught another day) and a large stripe (which we all enjoyed for dinner that night). Thankfully, we spent the afternoon on the boat and not in the hospital.

It was a trip that I will never forget. After all, how could I with a knot in my right jaw and a mild case of TMJ to remind me daily of Drew's first Guntersville catch.

About six months later, Drew and I were back on Guntersville throwing square bill crankbaits and floating worms in and around fallen trees. I was in the front of the boat when I heard a splash. Drew had hooked a nice bass. I was watching closely when suddenly the fish came off the hook and Drew's crankbait went flying out of the water at my head. I turned just as the crankbait hooks buried into my left jaw between my ear and my eye.

Drew sounded like his dog had just died when he whispered, "Not again." Luckily, the hook was not buried to the barb, and it popped right out. We both had a good laugh and went back to fishing.

Drew and I have now fished together many times in many different places. We have caught largemouth, smallmouth, spots, peacock bass, crappie, bream, baby tarpon, white bass, yellow bass, stripers, trout, stingrays, bluefish, and many others. Thankfully, he hasn't caught me again.

In all my life fishing, only one person has hooked me in the face…and Drew did it twice in six months.

The Fishing Nut showing off the stripe he caught after catching me

12
Charlie 2 Shot

Within ten minutes after I met Charles, he informed me that the suit I was wearing looked like crap, that I needed help in the way I dressed, and that I should exercise more. During that same period, I asked Charles when he would come to the realization that he was a lot older than he thought and not near as pretty. We immediately became great friends.

At some point, our first conversation morphed from jokes and criticisms to our mutual love for the outdoors. Charles had grown up hunting and fishing in Mississippi and glowed as he reflected on childhood trips with his father. Charles also longed for the opportunity to return to the woods. By the end of the evening, Charles and I were planning our first hunting trip together for the following year.

Charles and I anxiously counted the days until our trip. As we waited, we often discussed our past experiences in the outdoors and made trips to a local sporting goods store. We were both about ready to pop during the weeks leading up to the hunt.

Charles and I decided to meet at the lodge adjacent to the land we would be hunting the afternoon before we planned to hunt. I thought we were meeting the day before our hunt so he could check his scope and get an early start the following morning. As soon as I looked in his truck, I realized that we needed to meet early just so he would have enough time to unload and unpack.

Charles had brought three hunting rifles (a .270, .280, and a 7mm-08), enough ammunition to shoot at every deer in the county, two large coolers, four duffel bags full of clothes, several pairs of boots, and every hunting gadget that was innovative and foolproof twenty years ago. Charles had brought enough clothes and provisions to survive months in the wilderness, all for a four-day hunting trip in Alabama. I have always had a reputation of bringing way too much stuff with me when I hunt, and Charles made me look like a minimalist. The jokes started before his truck was unloaded.

After we finally finished unloading, we put on a pot of venison chili and went outside to make sure every gun in his arsenal was hitting the target. I kept asking Charles if it was really necessary to have three guns. He finally responded "Look, you never know." I immediately quipped back, "You can only shoot one at a time – you either can't shoot or you've upset the wrong person."

Any confidence I had in Charles faded when I noticed that his .270 appeared to be fifty years' old with a half inch of dust on it, his .280 had a cracked stock, and his 7mm-08 had a new scope and wasn't even bore sighted. I asked Charles, "Do you need all these guns to throw at the deer or bludgeon them?" He didn't find me funny. He still doesn't.

After looking over all of the guns and considering the pros, cons, and obstacles, Charles decided to hunt with his old .270. I agreed with his decision, assuming the .270 could actually fire without blowing up or falling apart.

I wanted to set a target at twenty yards just to make sure it was hitting the paper, but Charles insisted that his first shot be at 100 yards. I reluctantly agreed and placed a target at 100 yards.

After wiping the dust off his gun, loading a round, commenting that his bolt needed oil, and bracing his gun, Charles was ready to take his first shot. A few moments later, Charles steadied the crosshairs and slowly squeezed his trigger. Thankfully, his gun fired. Unfortunately, neither of us could find the hole on the target with our binoculars.

Charles proceeded to make excuses for his gun and his shooting. I proceeded to point out the positives (including that the gun didn't backfire and kill him) and the negatives (primarily his gun and his shooting).

After a few minutes of back and forth, we decided to walk to his target to see if we had missed the hole with our binoculars. We were both shocked when we walked up to the target and realized that the reason we hadn't seen the hole with our binoculars was because the hole was in the one place neither of us expected, in the center of the small black ring in the middle of the target.

Charles had hit a bullseye with the first shot through his antique .270 with a scope from the cold war era. He declared his .270 ready to hunt and said his next shot would be at a deer.

As he was strutting back from the target, Charles looked over at me and confidentially said, "You have been railing on me all day – I hope you realize from now on that I've got this." I chuckled and responded, "Congratulations, you killed a sheet of paper – let's see how you do when a deer walks out." Charles was laughing when he hit me on the top of my shoulder twice and joked, "The paper is fine, I just made one small hole in the bullseye."

Since it had only taken thirty or so minutes to check his .270 (one minute to take a shot and twenty-nine minutes to laugh at each other), we decided to head back to camp to get everything packed up and ready for the morning hunt.

To me, getting ready for the morning hunt meant loading the backpack and laying out layers in the order I would put them on in the morning. I finished preparing the gear and had been sitting at the table for several minutes when I finally yelled at Charles to make sure he was OK.

A few minutes later, Charles walked out in full camouflage. Apparently, to Charles, getting ready for the morning hunt meant trying on all of his clothes and modeling them.

As soon as he walked out, I proceeded to tell him that his old camouflage looked like crap, that he needed help in the way he dressed, and that he should exercise more if he wanted to wear size medium clothes. We both had a good laugh about how things had changed from the night when we first met each other.

A little while later, we sat down at the table to enjoy a big pot of chili and an abundance of stories and laughs. Throughout dinner, Charles let me have it for everything I said about him and his gun. I had earned everything he said and took it in stride.

As the evening was coming to a close and we were preparing to call it a night, we started planning which stands to hunt the following morning. Charles wanted to hunt in a shooting house that overlooked two long fields on a gas line. I decided to join Charles instead of hunting since I had the fortune of a full freezer from bow season. We then called it a night and tried to get some sleep despite the anticipation and excitement.

We awoke early the following morning and left for the woods well before sunrise. After creeping through thick pine rows for what seemed like miles, we finally entered the stand.

We settled in and opened the windows for the morning hunt. We were dead still and quiet for a little under three minutes before the joking and laughing started. We quickly closed the windows to hopefully avoid scaring every deer in the county.

On one hand, the closed windows did wonders to limit the sound. On the other hand, closed windows in a small, airtight shooting house following a night of chili is truly a terrible idea.

About an hour after sunrise, we were faced with a true dilemma. Our options were to (1) go back to camp; (2) stay in the shooting house with the windows open and likely spook all of the deer from the sound and the smell; or (3) stay in the close quarters of the shooting house and choke. We went back to camp.

During breakfast, we decided to hunt in the same stand that afternoon to hopefully catch a rutting buck looking for does. An hour or so after breakfast, we made our way back to the shooting house we had hunted in that morning and prepared for a long hunt.

Thankfully, we were able to keep the windows shut without issue on the afternoon sit. During the first hour of the hunt, we saw a few does and a young one-horned buck, but the action was limited throughout most of the afternoon.

Late that afternoon, we were diligently scanning both fields intently trying to catch movement when, behind a pine tree to our left, I saw the front leg of a deer and what I thought were his grey antlers. When I told Charles there was a deer to our left and that I thought it was a good buck, he laughed and accused me of thinking every limb, blade of grass, and animal that moved was a deer with antlers. While there may have been some truth to his accusations, I knew that I had seen a deer.

Charles continued to watch the field to his right when the deer I thought I had seen stepped into the clearing. As soon as I noticed the deer, I elbowed Charles in the ribs and whispered, "There he is – I told you so." We both slowly turned to our left and pulled up our binoculars to look at the deer.

We realized at the same time that the deer in the field was an amazing ten-point buck that was definitely old and mature enough to take. It was also the biggest buck that Charles had ever seen on stand while hunting.

We immediately went from jovial and picking at each other to silent hunters on a mission. We quietly opened the window to the left and Charles slowly grabbed the old .270, extended the barrel out the window, and rested the old wooden stock on the window ledge.

The intensity was palpable as Charles shouldered his rifle and looked through his scope at the buck. The regal buck was standing broadside at just under 150 yards. Unfortunately, the only part of the buck that wasn't blocked by a pine limb was his head and each and every one of his ten points.

We watched the skittish buck in silence for several minutes as he slowly stepped into the clearing in front of the steep embankment at the back of the field. Our anxiety increased exponentially with every second that passed. After what felt like hours, the buck finally stepped out to where Charles had a clear shot.

Charles slowly rested his cheek on the stock of his rifle and raised his right hand to the trigger. As he prepared to shoot, the buck took a step toward us, and the perfect broadside shot turned into a terrible quartering to shot that would have been unethical because of the angle of the deer and the likelihood of wounding him.

The waiting game started again, and our anxiety increased with each passing moment. Finally, the buck took a step back and was now standing at a perfect quartering away angle in front of the hill.

Charles again rested his cheek on his .270, braced his left arm, and steadied the crosshairs behind the buck's shoulder. Charles then whispered, "I've got him" and flipped his safety.

I was watching the buck through binoculars as Charles squeezed the trigger of his old .270 for the second time in two days. The explosion of his gun was immediately followed by the unmistakable thud of the bullet hitting.

The buck jumped, took several steps to the right, glanced at the hill where the bullet had buried in a cloud of dust as it flew clear over his back, looked up at the shooting house where we sat with our mouths open in shock and disappointment, and then he trotted into the woods.

Charles had hunted his entire life and is extremely confident with a rifle. However, he had succumbed to a severe case of buck fever and missed the biggest buck of his life.

Charles was shaking his head in devastation and utter disappointment as he slowly turned to me and asked, "What happened?" I knew Charles was very upset and needed support and words of encouragement. Unfortunately for him, he was sitting with me, and we generally picked at each other at every possible opportunity.

I gave Charles a comforting pat on the shoulder, nodded gingerly, and whispered, "Good shot." Charles stopped shaking his head and gave me a look that made it clear what he thought of me at that moment.

Charles turned back to where the deer had been standing and whispered several things that I couldn't understand. One thing that was abundantly clear was that he couldn't believe he missed. Not knowing what else to say or do, I leaned over and whispered, "Do you want me to take the shot if he walks back out?" Charles responded, "That isn't funny." Charles didn't find much of what I had to say about his shot funny.

After a few minutes of good spirited humor directed at Charles, he said he was done for the day and wanted to go back to the camp.

Once we made our way back to camp, I joked that Charles should either borrow my rifle or use one of the other guns in his arsenal. All Charles said in response was, "Let's go shoot." Charles suspected (or hoped) that the scope on his .270 had somehow miraculously come off zero.

Charles set up and took another shot with his .270. We pulled up our binoculars and saw that his bullet had hit the edge of the bullseye very close to where his first shot had hit the day before. As soon as I saw the shot, I said, "Yep, the gun was definitely the problem – it couldn't have been you."

To kill time, Charles decided to zero his 7mm-08. I suggested that we set the paper at twenty yards to see where he was hitting on paper before moving out. Charles was adamant that we shoot the rifle that wasn't even bore sighted at 100 yards just to see what would happen.

Charles sat the gun on the vice, steadied the scope, and pulled the trigger. The bullet hit the edge of the paper over a foot away from the bullseye. We were both surprised he had even hit paper.

Charles asked me how many clicks I thought he should adjust his scope. I estimated the number of inches that the bullet had missed the bullseye, multiplied it by four, and then added a few for good measure. I told Charles, "Move the scope sixty-one clicks up and four to the left." Puzzled, Charles asked, "Are you serious?" I responded confidently, "Absolutely, it's just math."

I was actually joking and had no idea what I was talking about, but I sounded extremely confident and believable. Charles wasn't completely fooled, but he made the adjustments I suggested to humor me. He then set his gun in the vice, steadied the crosshairs on the bullseye, and pulled the trigger.

I tried to hide the shock when I looked through the binoculars and saw that the bullet was within the bullseye ring. Without pulling down the binoculars, I made it very clear to Charles that I knew exactly what I was talking about (I didn't). We had a good laugh as he took several more shots to verify that we had zeroed a new scope that wasn't bore sighted in just two shots, which we had.

For the first time since I had met Charles, he had very little to say the remainder of the night. I, on the other hand, was anything but quiet. I hazed Charles every few moments, continuously reminding him of his keen hunting abilities and his stellar shooting. Charles called it a night right after dinner.

I awoke early the next morning as I often do in hunting camp to recharge my batteries and reflect on things. To my surprise, Charles was awake and fully dressed. I don't know if he slept at all the night before, but he was clearly on a mission.

He looked up at me with bloodshot eyes and said, "I'm taking my new gun and we are going to get that deer." I responded, "Great, – so you are going to let me shoot this time." Charles sternly responded, "No – you aren't funny." I replied, "Fine, but make sure you bring plenty of ammo – you need it." He declared that I still wasn't funny, and we were on our way to sit in the same shooting house where he had missed the giant ten-point the previous evening.

You could feel the energy in the shooting house as the sun broke over the trees that morning. We both watched intently as we mistook every limb in the woods as antlers. Every few minutes, I would say, "There he is" just to mess with Charles. He didn't find it funny.

About an hour after sunrise, Charles saw movement to our right. I felt my heart in my throat when I heard Charles whisper, "There he is." We were watching the woodline with our binoculars when we both saw the buck clearly.

There, standing approximately 200 yards away on the edge of the field was a mature eight-point buck with slightly curled main beams. I whispered, "Get your gun." Charles didn't move. Frustrated, I asked, "What are you doing?" All he said was, "That isn't him."

We proceeded to argue for several minutes over whether he should take the buck, but Charles was adamant that he was only interested in shooting one deer, his deer, and that he would rather enjoy the experience and go home emptyhanded than shoot any other buck. I told Charles that I disagreed with him, but I truly appreciated and respected his decision.

We saw a few more does that morning and one very small buck. Unfortunately, we didn't see his ten point. After a great hunt that morning, we headed back to camp to eat a quick breakfast before heading back for a long sit that afternoon.

At breakfast, we reflected on our first afternoon hunt. Charles had gone from cautiously optimistic to being realistic. He knew that he had missed his chance at a once-in-a-lifetime buck, and he was kicking himself because of it.

Toward the end of breakfast, Charles, who was very dejected, said he wasn't going to hunt that afternoon and that I should go instead. I love messing with Charles, I really do, but at that moment he needed encouragement instead of good hearted jokes and criticism.

I refused to hunt and insisted that we sit in the spot one last time as a team in case the buck walked back out. Our conversation then shifted to discussing how the buck hadn't been that spooked at the miss and that he could potentially make another appearance that afternoon. Charles had gone full circle and was now back to being excited and determined.

We went back to the stand just after breakfast and prepared for a long afternoon.

We were sitting quietly in the stand when I nudged Charles, pointed to our right, and whispered, "Look right there." Charles immediately perked up and started frantically scanning the edge of the field where I had pointed. I leaned over and pointed again and said, "Isn't that an awesome bird." He didn't see the humor, but we were back in our usual routine.

Every few minutes during our afternoon sit, I would say "There he is", "I see him," or something else to mess with Charles. The first few times, Charles sat up and became excited. He quickly became immune to the jokes.

As the sun started to creep behind the Southern pines, Charles and I started quietly discussing how much we had enjoyed the memorable hunt. While Charles was understandably upset that he had missed the trophy ten-point buck, he was mainly thankful for the experience, the opportunity, and the comradery.

In between the jabs and the jokes, we both had tried to be optimistic about the possibility that the buck would make a second appearance and give Charles a second shot. However, neither of us believed it would happen.

We were about to call it a day and head back to the camp when, for the 42nd time that day, I whispered, "Get your gun." Charles knew from the urgency and excitement in my tone that I wasn't joking, and he quickly looked out the window and slowly grabbed his new rifle. There, standing approximately 150 yards on the ridge, was the same ten-point buck that Charles had missed the previous day.

The atmosphere in the shooting house was electric when Charles saw the buck for the second time. We were both trying to control our nerves and emotions as our adrenalin and excitement turned the frigid January afternoon turned into July in the tropics.

I don't know which of us was shaking more as Charles slowly extended the barrel of his new 7mm-08 out the window, rested the synthetic stock on the ledge of the shooting house, braced his left arm on his knee and his right arm on the other window ledge, rested his cheek on the rifle, and steadied the crosshairs on the buck. I was holding my breath trying to hold the binoculars steady when Charles whispered, "I've got him" and squeezed the trigger. For the second time in two days, Charles had shot at the biggest buck of his life.

Charlie 2 Shot preparing for the shot

The boom of the gun was immediately followed by the buck once again jumping and leaving the field. It wasn't clear if Charles was asking a question or making a statement when he turned to me and said, "I got him." I erased any doubt when I exclaimed, "Oh yea, you got him!"

We were trying desperately to contain our emotion and excitement as we sat in the stand waiting to go mark where Charles had shot the buck to help us recover the deer later that night.

We both agreed to wait about an hour before looking for the deer. About ten minutes into our wait, Charles looked at me and whispered, "Do you think it's been long enough? I do." I grinned and responded, "Absolutely – lets go."

What started as stealthily creeping up the ridge turned into a jog as we approached where the buck had been standing. As soon as we arrived to the spot, Charles saw the big ten-point just on the edge of the woods a few yards away. When we realized the impossible had happened, our whispers and uncertainty turned into celebration, screams of excitement, triumph, and, most importantly, thankfulness for the opportunity.

The next few minutes were surreal as we celebrated the hunt and the deer. Charles was sitting underneath a pine tree admiring and thanking the deer when I looked at him and said, "You know, your shot was a little low – maybe if you averaged the two you would have one good shot." Without missing a beat, Charles responded, "I'm glad I missed the first shot – I wouldn't trade this for anything." At that moment, Charles became, and will always be, Charlie 2 Shot to me.

That hunt with Charlie 2 Shot is one of my all-time favorite and most memorable hunting trips, and I didn't pull the trigger or even take a rifle with me to the woods.

Charles and I have reflected on that trip many times, and we both agree that the memories and bonds that were made during that trip are far more special than any deer that we could ever take, even on the second shot.

13
One of Those Days

Occasionally, the stars align, the wind and weather cooperate, and the fish only seem to be interested in eating the lure on the end of your line. These rare, special, and unpredictable days are few and far between and typically end with sore thumbs, a few what-ifs, and at least one story about one that got away. These days can build and define lifetime bonds with fishing buddies.

Ben and I drove to the cabin on Lake Guntersville late on a muggy Friday afternoon in July to meet my family for a weekend at the lake. We arrived before everyone else and planned to fish the Cove around the boathouse until Mom, Dad, and Sunni arrived with Wildcat cheeseburgers, onion rings, and strawberry milkshakes from Charburger in Guntersville.

On this particular evening, we were rigged with Strike King triple wing buzzbaits. Ben's buzzbait was chartreuse and white, and mine was a semi-homemade special I had modified by painting the head black and changing the skirt to black, brown and purple.

We had just pulled out of the boat house when I threw the lure for the first time, a long cast that gently landed next to a large fallen tree. I engaged the reel and started working the buzzbait back to the boat. The buzzbait was gurgling on top of the water just in front of the tree limbs when, all of a sudden, a bass ferociously exploded out of the water attacking the lure. I immediately yanked the rod back as hard as I could and prepared for the fight.

Unfortunately, the buzzbait, as it flew over our heads and hit the boathouse behind me, was more likely to hook one of the grey bats that fly around Guntersville at dusk than a largemouth bass.

As I reeled in the slack line, I told Ben, "I missed that fish on purpose – catching a fish on the first cast is a curse and ruins the trip." Ben told me that he didn't believe me in a manner that would have made the saltiest sailor proud.

As we shared a laugh, I repositioned the boat where Ben couldn't cast at the tree where I had missed the fish. As soon as he realized what I was doing, he proceeded to tell me exactly what he thought of me and the maneuver, again, in a manner that would have made a sailor proud.

Ben continued his tirade as my second cast landed in the same spot as the first. I was listening closely to the buzzbait churning on the surface while I responded to Ben in an appropriate manner. I was hoping to hear the splash of a fish striking the lure. Instead, I heard a sound remarkably similar to an overweight, hairy man doing a cannonball in the shallow end of a crowded pool.

I squared my shoulders toward the explosion, reeled down to take the slack out of the line, and then channeled every bit of strength possible as I ripped my rod back to set the hook. This time, however, I connected with the fish, and the fight was on.

The only words spoken during the fight were, "Get the net!" A few minutes later, Ben swung the giant largemouth into the bottom of the old Fisher aluminum bass boat. As Ben reached down to lip the fish, I stopped him and told him that big fish are sometimes difficult to handle and that I didn't want him to drop the fish. I was in awe as I lifted the hawg.

As I admired the bass, I struggled to estimate her weight. She was very long, almost twenty-four inches, but she was also a little skinny, particularly around the tail. The bass had a large mouth that could easily cover my fist. Ben and I both estimated the bass between eight and nine pounds before we weighed the fish. The Deliar scale disagreed and read just over seven pounds. I always hated that scale.

One of those days with Ben!

Instead of releasing the bass in the lake, I turned on the pumps to the livewell to hold the bass to show the family when they arrived. After putting the fish in the livewell, Ben and I continued fishing the Cove.

We caught numerous largemouth between four and five and a half pounds over the next hour and a half of that unforgettable afternoon. We kept the biggest four fish we had caught, in the livewell.

The family arrived at the cabin right at dark. As soon as they pulled up, Dad hurried down to the dock and shouted, "Y'all caught anything?" I yelled back, "Our biggest five weigh around twenty-five pounds, and I have one over seven pounds." As he was laughing, I pulled the seven-pounder and another bass that weighed right at five pounds out of the livewell. Ben followed with the other two fish in the livewell.

Dad was shocked at the catch and kept asking how we had caught the fish. I told him that everything had fallen into place and that it was just one of those days. We released all four bass and went to the cabin to eat our Charburger dinner.

During dinner, we made a plan to fish throughout the night. The plan consisted of throwing spinnerbaits with Colorado blades and Zoom speed worms. We quickly ate and went back out on the water.

We threw spinnerbaits in the same area where we had caught the fish before dark on buzzbaits. The conditions were perfect, and we covered every inch of water where we had caught fish earlier. Unfortunately, we did not get a single bite. After a few hours of pounding the same area, we finally decided to move to deeper water to throw the worms.

We drove to a transition area where the water goes from twenty feet up to ten feet. We then turned on a black light and started throwing the worms along the ridge. Between the willow flies, the grey bats, the bugs, and the heat, it was a struggle to fish, especially considering we were not getting any bites, other than from mosquitos.

After fishing for several hours, we started reminiscing about our afternoon, which felt like it had occurred in a different lifetime.

We had fished for almost five hours without a bite when Ben yelled, "I've got a monster." I continued working the worm assuming that Ben was lying until I heard the drag on his spinning reel. I quickly reeled in the lure and went to the back of the boat to help and heckle him.

As I watched Ben fight the fish, I commented, "That fish is staying down – it's a trash fish, either a drum or a flathead." Struggling with the fish, Ben grunted, "It's a bass, a monster bass."

I was standing next to Ben holding the net and telling him to hurry up with the trash fish so we could get back to fishing when, unexpectedly, the fish exploded out of the water right next to the boat, confirming Ben's proclamation. The second the fish broke the water, I screamed, "IT'S A BASS!" and instinctively swung the net as the bass returned to the water without fear, logic, or hesitation.

As soon as I lifted the net out of the water, I realized that I had landed Ben's bass, the bass of a lifetime. I laid the net with the gargantuan bass on the front deck of the boat. We turned on our flashlights to marvel at the beast.

I had fished my entire life and had never seen a bass like the one Ben caught. To this day, I have never seen another bass the size of Ben's fish. I had caught a bass that weighed just over seven pounds earlier in the evening, and Ben's fish made mine look small. I have caught two bass over nine pounds, and neither of those fish remotely compared to this one. Ben had caught the holy grail of bass, and, for the first time that night, we were speechless.

After a few moments, I told Ben that it was best if I pulled the bass out of the net since she was tangled, I had a lot more experience handling big fish, and he might drop her. Ben reluctantly agreed. The truth is that opportunities to hold a fish of that magnitude are rare, and I wanted to hold the fish first, even though it bit the wrong worm.

My hand felt tiny when I first lipped the bass. Instead of lifting the fish, I put her gently back in the net. I then made a fist with my right hand and easily inserted it into the mouth of Ben's monster. As soon as we saw that my fist fit easily, Ben commented, "I bet you can fit two fists in her mouth." In a condescending tone, I said, "Naw" and attempted to insert my left fist as well. For the second time that night, I had substantially underestimated Ben's bass. Both of my fists fit in the mouth of Ben's bass.

With the eagerness and excitement of a young child who had just received his first bicycle and a puppy in the same day, Ben said, "Alright, hand her to me." I reached down, lipped the bass with both hands, and then lifted the bass completely out of the net.

On one hand, I was jealous that Ben had caught the bass of my dreams. Moreso, I was just grateful that I was able to be a part of the experience.

As I took a step toward Ben to hand him his fish, the fish bucked like an angry one ton bull being ridden for the first time. I tried desperately to hold on to Ben's bass. I'm not sure if it was the weight or strength of Ben's bass, the fact that I was tired from fishing all afternoon and night, or me choking in the moment, but I dropped Ben's bass in the middle of the front deck of the boat.

Ben's bass fell in slow motion, and all we could do was watch and scream an elongated "NOOOOOOO" like a bad movie. As quickly as Ben's bass hit the deck, she snapped to her left and went crashing back in the dark waters of Lake Guntersville.

Fortunately, Ben's bass was still hooked and he was still holding his rod. Unfortunately, Ben's line sounded like a shotgun when it snapped.

We both sat on the deck of the boat in silence and in shock. After a few minutes, I broke the silence and said, "Man, I'm really sorry." Ben responded, "It's OK, – how much do you think she weighed?" I didn't tell him that night, and I still haven't.

The mood was somber until I asked him, "Do you want to throw me in the lake?" We then shared a good laugh and called it a night.

As soon as we got back to the dock, I ran to the cabin to wake Dad up to tell him about the fish. When he saw our excitement, he knew that something special had happened.

I was reliving every aspect of the story to Dad and was to the point where I netted the fish when Dad anxiously interrupted me and exclaimed, "I wanna see the fish!" Ben spoke up and joked, "Yeah, me, too."

Dad was obviously confused by Ben's comment and asked, "What do you mean?" Ben chimed in and said, "Corey chunked the fish in the lake to make sure that no one could say that they caught a bigger fish in his boat." Ben then said he was just thankful for the experience and didn't care about losing the fish. Dad, however, berated me.

Sometime during the night, Ben realized the magnitude of what had happened. He did not talk at breakfast the next morning and had a sick look on his face. He finally asked, "Have you ever caught a fish anywhere near that big?" I grimaced and said, "Nope." I thought he was going to vomit when I continued and said, "I don't know anyone else that has, either."

Ben then shook his head in disgust and said, "You know I'll never let you forget that I caught the biggest fish in your boat and you chunked it back in the water." I laughed and said, "I wouldn't expect you to."

Ben has held true to his word and has never let me forget his fish. To this day, he still reminds me of that night on a regular basis. It was truly one of those days that I will never forget, even though I would like to at times.

14
Pass the Sausage

If I enjoy something, I want those around me to know about it and also have the opportunity to experience the enjoyment. A prime example is the outdoors.

I have introduced numerous people to hunting and fishing. There is no describing the excitement and satisfaction when you help land a new fisherman's first bass or feel the shooting house shake the first time a deer materializes in front of a new hunter.

One of my favorite experiences introducing someone to hunting was my good friend Clark's first hunting trip.

I first mentioned hunting to Clark as I was wiping tears from my eyes from laughing at the story of his hiking trip in the Montana mountains and how he avoided the bears by occasionally yelling, "HEY BEAR!"

Clark had never hunted, but he was very interested in trying it. I told him a few of us were going deer hunting the next January, that we would love for him to go, and that he could use my rifle and borrow my camo. He jumped at the opportunity.

A few months later, it was time for our trip. We arrived at camp late in the afternoon on a cold January day. We had timed the trip around the time deer rut in Alabama, and we all had high hopes.

Since Clark was borrowing my rifle, I wanted to make sure that the scope was accurate and that he was comfortable with the gun. Clark gave me a puzzled look when I handed him the rifle and ammo. I knew that Clark had never hunted for deer, but I had no idea that he had also never shot a deer rifle. Clark and I spent some time discussing the .270 and how to use and shoot the rifle.

Once I was comfortable that he had a firm grasp of the rifle (and its safety), Clark loaded the gun and took a shot at the target sitting 100 yards away. I pulled up binoculars to see if Clark had hit his target. I tried to hide the shock and amazement when I told Clark that he hit a bullseye. I then walked him through unloading and reloading the rifle and told him to take another shot.

Clark's next shot, his second shot ever with a deer rifle, hit the edge of the hole from his first shot, also in the bullseye. When I told Clark his second shot was also perfect, he unloaded the rifle and handed it back to me. Puzzled, I asked, "Don't you want to shoot some more." He shook his head and said, "If I keep shooting, I may miss." I didn't argue with him, and we headed back to camp to prepare for dinner.

At dinner, Clark's excitement and anticipation reminded me of a teenage boy preparing for his first date. Every time someone shared a nugget of information, Clark would nod eagerly as he took mental notes and learned as much as possible. He became visibly more excited the more we talked that evening.

Clark took in every bit of advice we offered, including shot placement and how to determine if a deer was mature enough to shoot. We also tried to temper his expectations by explaining most hunts don't end with a deer on the ground and that a successful hunt isn't defined by a kill.

One of the other guys in the camp asked Clark what he would do if he shot a deer. Clark energetically responded, "I want to eat it, especially the sausage!" Clark, in a troubled tone, then said, "I really hope I don't shoot him in the sausage."

Everyone went silent trying to figure out if he was being serious. I then asked, "Clark, exactly where is the sausage." He responded, "I don't know, but I sure don't want to shoot it, because that's my favorite meat." Everyone began laughing hysterically and did not stop laughing until after dinner. I believe that was the hardest I had laughed up to that point of my life. Once everyone calmed down, we explained deer sausage to Clark.

The next morning, we woke to temperatures in the high teens and ice covering the ground. We all went to different stands before sunrise and sat patiently until mid-morning.

We met back at the camp for breakfast after the morning hunt. The deer had not moved that morning. I was worried that the lack of deer would derail Clark's excitement, but he had enjoyed the sunrise and watching the squirrels and birds. He said he had loved everything, except for the cold. I told him that I would give him warm clothes for the afternoon to help with the cold.

Before we went back to the stands after lunch, I gave Clark my thick Realtree coat. He thanked me and went to the stand.

An hour or so before dark, I heard a shot from the area where Clark was hunting. A few minutes later, Clark messaged that he had shot his first deer, a nice buck. Clark stayed in the stand until we arrived a little after dark.

When we pulled up, Clark was standing next to his shooting house. The first thing I noticed was his smile – which extended from ear-to-ear. I then noticed that Clark wasn't wearing the Realtree coat I had loaned him. Instead, he was wearing a giant bright blue ski parka.

Clark was the first and only person I've ever seen hunt in a bright blue ski coat, and I couldn't help but laugh at him. I asked in a confused tone, "Why aren't you wearing the camo coat I gave you?" Convinced nothing was out of the ordinary, he responded in his normal conversational tone, "I am – it's just under my blue coat."

We laughed hysterically at Clark. Clark didn't mind the laughter and barrage of jokes about the camo and his blue coat. After all, he had just shot his first buck and was as happy as I had ever seen anyone in my life.

After standing around and discussing Clark's shot for a few minutes, we all walked to the spot where Clark said the deer was standing when he shot. As soon as we arrived, I looked at Clark, turned and looked at the shooting house, and then asked, "Are you sure this is where he was standing?" Clark nodded eagerly and confidently said, "Yeah, absolutely – no doubt he was standing right here." I then asked Clark if he knew that the shot had been close to 175 yards. He asked me if that was good. I responded, "I'll let you know when we find the deer."

We looked in the field but never found blood. Clark showed us exactly where he thought the deer ran in the woods. We all questioned him, but he was confident and had no doubt. We looked around the entrance in the woods but again didn't find blood.

At this point, everyone but Clark was coming to the realization that Clark likely missed the deer or had made a bad shot. We continued searching for blood in the field and down the main trail coming off the field, but there was no sign of blood or the deer.

We were standing about twenty yards down the trail off of the field when one of the guys made the comment that we should consider giving up for the night and looking for the deer the next morning. At that point, Charles (also known as Charlie 2 Shot) spoke up and said loftily, "I'm fine coming back tomorrow, but it probably isn't necessary since the deer is right there." We were standing less than five feet from Clark's deer.

I do not recall ever seeing anyone as excited as Clark was when he first saw his deer. I will never forget Clark and the look on his face as he sat next to the deer in his bright blue ski jacket holding the deer's antlers. Sharing that experience with Clark ranks near the top of my all-time favorite experiences in the outdoors.

When Clark asked me about his shot, I told him that he had made a perfect quartering away shot, that he could not have hit the deer any better, and that it was a very quick kill. I also explained that the only reason we hadn't found blood was because he did not get an exit wound on the deer because of the angle of the shot. Clark remarked, "I'm really glad – I did everything you said, but I was nervous and really shaking." I patted Clark on the back and said, "Clark, you did good buddy – and you didn't even hit him in the sausage."

After several pictures, a few laughs, and a lot of pats on the back and thattaboys, we were ready to drag the deer back to the field and load him up. Wanting to be involved and help as much as possible, Clark asked, "Where should I grab him." I told him the best place to grab a buck, particularly a rutting buck, is around his back legs, specifically where the legs are solid black (from urinating on his tarsal glands and rubbing his legs together, which I didn't mention to Clark). I also told Clark that he would need to squeeze the black area of the back legs as hard as he could to keep the deer from slipping and then to drag him out backwards.

I was completely joking with Clark. After all, the last place you want to grab a rutting buck is the back of the legs because of the rancid stench. I didn't think he would take me seriously given the rank smell, but he had a firm grasp of the back legs before I could stop him and had his buck halfway to the field. Charles and I raced to catch up to Clark, laughing the entire way.

Once we had Clark's buck back to the field, we lifted him into the back of the Polaris Ranger. Charles, Clark, and I then jumped in and started back to camp. As soon as we took off, I noticed that Clark had a strange look on his face. I turned to him and asked, "What's wrong?" He grimaced slightly and said, "What is that smell?" I couldn't help but laugh as I responded, "Is it your hands?" Clark pulled his hands up to his nose, took a deep whiff, and then nearly gagged as he exclaimed, "Why in the world do my hands smell like that?" Charles and I almost fell out of the Ranger laughing when Clark realized the stench on his hands resulted from his grabbing the rutting buck's back legs.

Charles and I then told Clark about the age old tradition of being "blooded" when you kill your first buck. Clark was so excited about his deer, he didn't care. He said he understood completely and that he wanted to make sure that he enjoyed the moment and honored and upheld every single tradition.

My love for playing pranks on people, especially people I really like, rivals my love of introducing people to the outdoors. As soon as Clark said he would honor every tradition, Charles and I started making up traditions. What started out as a little prank quickly spiraled out of control.

I told Clark that, generally, the hunter gets to choose his method of being blooded. Charles and I proceeded to describe the options for Clark, which included having a bucket of blood, organs, and guts dumped on the hunter, gargling the buck's private parts, and a few other options that should never be repeated.

At this point, Clark suspected that Charles and I were messing with him. We knew that we had to act quickly, or we would lose the golden opportunity.

Charles and I fed off of each other and both told Clark that we didn't blame him for not wanting to go with the other options and that we had made the same choice with our first bucks. We then explained to Clark that we had both chosen to stick our heads in the body cavity and "motorboat" the deer. Charles then told Clark that everyone in Mississippi chooses to motorboat his first buck. Charles and I were very convincing, especially to Clark.

We arrived back at camp and were in the process of field dressing Clark's deer to make sure we preserved the meat so that Clark could have his sausage. During the process, we continued discussing traditions and the importance of Clark honoring the tradition by motorboating the deer.

Clark kept saying, "Naw ... Naw" over and over, but he obviously was struggling with the situation. It didn't help that, by this point, everyone at camp was chanting "MO-TOR BOAT" repeatedly.

I like to think that Charles and I would normally stop Clark if he actually started to stick his head in the deer's cavity, but we were really enjoying messing with Clark in the moment. Charles and I kept explaining to Clark that it was a tradition, and that he really didn't want to be the one to ignore a tradition.

In about .3 seconds, Clark changed from shaking his head and screaming "Naw" over and over to being dead serious. Before Charles or I could stop him, Clark dropped his head and quickly approached the hanging deer like he was going to ram the deer's cavity with his head. Clark's forehead was just inside the cavity when the smell became too much. He had a red nose as he yanked his head back gagging. Everyone at camp laughed hysterically, even harder than the night before when Clark said he hoped he didn't shoot the deer in the sausage.

Any question that Clark may have had about whether Charles and I were serious, ended when he saw that we were both on the ground laughing so hard we were almost hyperventilating. About that time, he also noticed that we were videoing the scene.

The next words out of Clark's mouth were, "You assholes, this shit is going to end up on Myspace." What made the situation even funnier was that Myspace had lost its popularity to Facebook several years prior to that night and no one there even had a Myspace account.

I swore to Clark that the video would not end up on Myspace (it didn't), and that I would never share the video with anyone that wasn't there that night (I haven't).

That night, Clark became the only person I've ever known to kill a buck at 175 yards on his first day hunting or to kill a buck with his third shot ever with a deer rifle. He is also the only person I've ever known to motorboat the deer afterwards.

Clark, Charles, and I have now hunted together several times. Clark still borrows my .270, which I now refer to as Clark's gun. He did retire his bright blue ski jacket and replace it with a Realtree coat, but I'm still hopeful that the blue jacket will be used again.

A few years ago, I was sitting next to Clark in a shooting house when he shot his second deer. He was every bit as excited when he shot his second deer as he was for his first. He also had the exact same smile and showed the same amount of excitement when he sat down next to his second buck, held his antlers for the first time, and thanked the deer. Astonishingly, he didn't shoot his second buck in the sausage either.

Clark with his blue coat and first buck!

Go afield with a good attitude, with respect for the forest and fields in which you walk. Immerse yourself in the outdoor experience. It will cleanse your soul and make you a better person.

Fred Bear

15
My Girls

From the first memory of my wife through childhood, junior high, high school, college, and beyond, I always referred to her simply as "Larn."

I first met Larn on a chilly winter afternoon in late February. I was a hair over three months old riding in the back of Mom's car as we pulled into Larn's driveway just as she and her family arrived home from the hospital after she was born. I had no idea at the time that she would be the love of my life or that she was to be the mother of our children.

Corey and Larn, "Best Friends"

Larn and I were raised in Hartselle, a small town in North Alabama. As with most small towns, people were generally friendly in Hartselle, you rarely met a stranger, and local news, secrets, and gossip were readily available at either of the local barber shops, any place that served coffee, Dairy Delite or Dairy Queen, the local ballfields, church, and a host of other places. Also, close friends in Hartselle were typically referred to using nicknames, such as "Ozzie," "Hodgey," "Big Guy," and "Nate." To this day, the contact for my wife in my cell phone is still, "Larn."

Larn and I developed a close bond at a young age and became best friends during high school. Except for a short one-week period before homecoming our freshman year when we "went together," our relationship was never anything other than a very close friendship. Larn would often joke that I would stand beside her on her wedding day, but in a dress as a bridesmaid.

Larn and Corey, "Prom Night!"

We remained close friends throughout college and graduate school and met for lunch or dinner as often as possible. On a spring day a little over twenty-four years after we first laid eyes on each other as infants, we finally realized that we were much more than friends.

What started as an innocent lunch at Jim 'N Nick's BBQ and a casual trip to the zoo eventually turned into discussions about forever. After we agreed that we were perfect for each other and should get married, we decided that we should probably date first.

Seven months later to the day, I was waiting in the living room in Larn's trailer in Auburn surrounded by flowers and resting on one knee when she unsuspectingly walked through her front door after class. Before she could say anything, I gazed deeply in her eyes, extended the wooden box with the marquise diamond ring, and asked, "Will you marry me?" I couldn't exactly make out her response, which sounded more like a scream from Chewbacca than a "Yes", but her answer was clear from the tears and the affectionate hug.

We were engaged a little over nine months before our wedding day. We had decided to abandon tradition and see each other before the ceremony for pictures. I was standing at the alter facing the cross when Larn walked behind me and put her hands over my eyes. I immediately turned and was mesmerized by her radiant beauty and the most magnificent ivory dress. We both had tears in our eyes as we embraced each other. As I was hugging Larn, she whispered, "I threw up this morning." I laughed and said, "Me, too."

Two hours later, we were announced as husband and wife in front of friends and family by Brent (or "Big Guy"), a dear and beloved friend, brother, teammate, and smelly junior high square dance partner (for Larn). Thankfully, I was wearing a tux and not a bridesmaid dress.

Corey and Larn, "Wedding Day!"

When Brent presented Mr. and Mrs. Jenkins to the congregation for the first time, Larn made a loud "whooping" sound. No one was expecting it, but everyone laughed.

At the reception, one of our favorite high school teachers gave us hugs and then joked that she was shocked that it was Larn that acted up at the wedding and not Brent or me. Larn laughed and said I brought it out of her.

There are many benefits to marrying your best friend that you have known since birth. Particularly, you don't have to explain your quirks, obsessions, and past. When Larn said "I do," she was fully aware of my deep passion and obsession for hunting, fishing, and the outdoors.

Shortly after moving into our first house, I started dropping hints that *we* needed to "invest" in a bass boat. Larn was hesitant at first, primarily because of her concern that she would not be able to park her car in our two-car garage if we bought a boat. After assuring her that I would find a used boat at a good price, that the boat would fit in the garage with plenty of room to spare for her Honda Accord, and that I would park my truck in the driveway, she greenlighted the purchase.

A few weeks later, we drove to Tennessee to pick up a used red and white Skeeter ZX-190. As I pulled away with the boat hooked to the truck, Larn commented that the boat was a lot bigger than she expected and that she thought it would fill the garage without leaving room for her car. I assured her that I had measured the garage and that I was positive that both the boat and her car would fit in the garage with room to spare.

A few hours later, I pulled past our driveway, cut the wheel sharply, slowly pushed the boat in the driveway at a steep angle through the garage, and stopped where the motor was just touching the back left corner of the garage. I breathed a sigh of relief as I looked through the rear view mirror and realized that the boat fit perfectly in the garage. I threw the truck into park and strutted confidently around the truck bed to unhook the boat.

When I turned the back corner of the truck, Larn was standing on the other side of the trailer with her arms crossed, obviously unhappy. I wasn't sure why she was upset until I looked to the right and realized the issue.

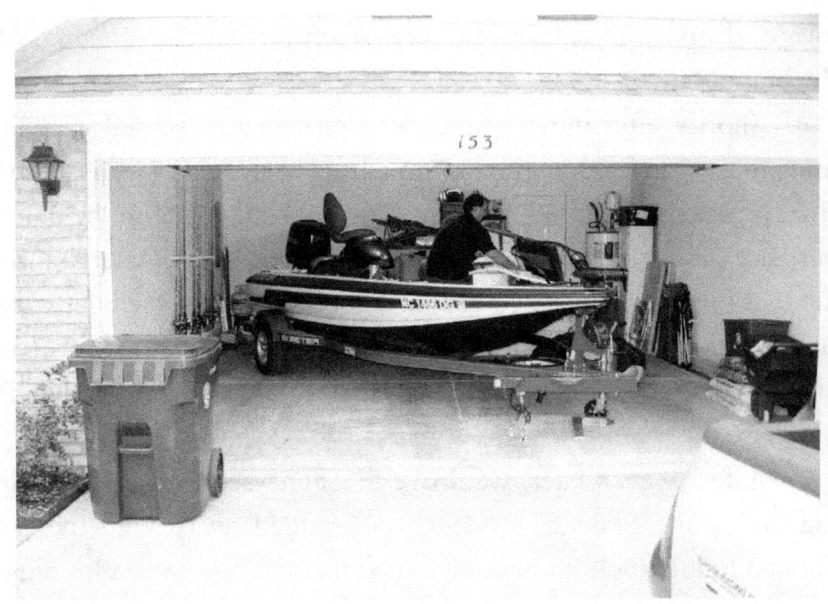

Oops! Where will we park Larn's Honda!?

The Skeeter and Larn's Honda would have absolutely both fit in garage, but only if we somehow took the boat off the trailer and removed the motor and the jack plate. Otherwise, the only way for Larn's car to fit in the garage with the boat would have been for her Honda to miraculously transform into a scooter, and it would have still been a tight fit.

It was painfully apparent how extremely unhappy Larn was that she no longer had a place to park in the garage. I profusely apologized for the miscalculation and sincerely offered to sell the boat or find somewhere else to store it. Larn laughed at the offer and, in her usual understanding tone, told me that she understood how much the boat meant to me and that she would be fine parking in the driveway next to my truck.

The following Saturday morning, we moved Larn's Honda out of the driveway and parked it on the road, hooked the boat up to the truck, and started the journey to my favorite ramp on Brown's Creek at Lake Guntersville. A little over an hour later, we were idling away from the dock for the first time in our new boat.

As soon as I was comfortable that we were far enough away from the dock to run the boat, I looked over at Larn and asked her if she was ready. Her excitement was obvious as she exclaimed, "Absolutely!"

Few boating experiences compare to the feeling when you come to plane for the first time in a new boat. I was relishing every second as I took a deep and relaxing breath, adjusted the seat slightly, pressed the throttle to the floor, and watched the water in front of the boat and the trees on the horizon.

I was expecting the motor's low growl to turn to a fierce roar as the boat lunged forward immediately coming to plane. Instead, the view of the horizon quickly changed from water and trees to solid grey carpet and the sun. The roar of the motor was little more than a whimper compared to Larn's screaming.

Instead of the quick and smooth plane I had expected, the boat had nearly flipped backwards. During the preparations, I had been so focused on taking in the experience and sharing it with Larn that I had completely forgotten to trim down the motor to fully submerge the prop at the correct angle before taking off. In the process, I had nearly thrown us into the lake and sunk our new boat.

The front of the boat, which had been facing skyward, dropped downward and slapped the water when I released the throttle, scaring Larn again. I then had the arduous task of explaining that I had accidentally forgotten to set the trim correctly before taking off and that I was not trying to play a joke on her.

Once she was somewhat convinced, I trimmed the motor all the way down, nervously pressed the throttle to the floor, and was thrown back in the seat as the boat jumped to plane.

I closed my eyes momentarily to feel the wind and to take in the moment. When I opened my eyes, I turned left to check on Larn. She had also closed her eyes and was leaning back in her seat with a grin across her face as she felt the wind in her hair and was enjoying the moment.

A few moments later, as we idled under the Highway 69 causeway, Larn looked at me with a grin, gave me an approving nod, patted me on my knee, and told me that she loved the boat and was very glad that we had it and that we could spend time together on the lake fishing. Her words sparked a multitude of emotions and feelings: deep pride, satisfaction, and enjoyment that the love of my life was eager to share my love of fishing and the outdoors and relief that she had forgiven me for kicking her out of the garage.

We fished in the Skeeter every time our hectic work schedules would allow. Larn picked up fishing very quickly and was throwing baitcasters, working lures, and fighting fish like a pro in no time.

We caught a lot of fish together. More importantly, we spent quality time together without distractions and strengthened our bond, friendship and marriage.

While fishing in the Skeeter, we would often discuss our goals, things we wanted to accomplish or experience, and our bucket lists. One afternoon, I mentioned to Larn that a life-long goal of mine was to bow hunt for bear. Larn immediately responded, "You can't go until you give me two kids!" I was initially taken aback by the fact that she was more concerned about having kids than me being mauled by a bear, but figured it was best for me to agree since she hadn't said no.

About a year after we purchased the Skeeter, we began discussing the possibility of expanding our family. After a lot of thought, discussion, and prayer, we agreed that we were ready for children.

Larn and I have always been obsessive-compulsive, goal-oriented planners. True to form, we established our ideal timeline and how we thought things should go. We hoped and prayed that we would be surprised with a plus symbol on the home pregnancy test within a few months, quickly find a new house with more room for our expanding family and a bigger garage to accommodate the Skeeter and the Honda, move and be settled before the beginning of the third trimester, and have a healthy baby within a year to a year and a half.

We thought that we had everything figured out. God had different plans.

Within a few months, we found and moved into the exact house we were looking for with room for our expanding family and a bigger garage. We immediately filled the garage with the Honda and the Skeeter. The nursery, however, remained vacant for several years.

In late January of 2010, we finally saw the plus sign that we had hoped and prayed for. The pregnancy was difficult, and every pinch, cramp, and discomfort resulted in fear and anxiety that something was wrong with Larn or the baby.

To make matters worse, I was very little help throughout the majority of the pregnancy. I spent the entire summer recovering from shoulder surgery to fix the rotator cuff tear that I had suffered early in the first trimester when I landed on my outstretched arm after an unsuccessful, unexplainable, and idiotic attempt at an epic, no-arms, no-hands, and perfectly balanced sit-up on a large exercise ball.

By the middle of the third trimester, we finally found our groove. Outside of her daily sickness, Larn generally felt great. I had also recovered enough from surgery to finally be some help around the house.

We had set up the nursery exactly as we wanted it, purchased or received every possible baby gadget, and had a stockpile of diapers. We were as ready as we could be for our baby's arrival. We were even to a point where we weren't afraid every time we saw the doctor for regular appointments and waited to hear the baby's heartbeat. We were counting down the days to the due date, and our excitement grew with each passing moment.

On a Friday afternoon around a month before the due date, the doctor and nurse walked into the patient room and explained to Larn and me that her blood pressure was elevated, that there were risks for her and the baby, and that it was necessary for her to go on bed rest.

Throughout the weekend, I hovered over Larn and checked her blood pressure hourly. By Sunday afternoon, it was evident that Larn's blood pressure was not falling as the doctor had hoped.

First thing Monday morning, Larn called the doctor's office. After discussing the weekend and her increasing blood pressure with the nurse, the nurse told us to be at the office in an hour. She also suggested that we bring our bags.

A few hours later, the doctor admitted Larn to the hospital and began the process of inducing labor, which was a long and difficult process.

A little before midnight the night before our first baby was born, Larn turned to me and commented that she couldn't believe that we were about to be guardians of a baby girl. Larn then closed her eyes and drifted off to sleep. I, however, sat on the rock solid hospital couch with my eyes the size of coke cans and my mouth dropped for most of the night contemplating her words.

As I sat there worrying about Larn and the baby and longing for the opportunity to hold our baby girl for the first time, I couldn't help but wonder about the many firsts that we would experience with our first baby girl: the first time she looked at me with her little blue eyes, smiled, and grasped my little finger; the look in her eyes when she said "Dada" for the first time; the sheer enjoyment as she played in her "ocean" for the first time and nearly hyperventilated because she was laughing so hard; the determination on her face each time that she pulled herself up on our couch, tried to take a step, and fell, and the look of pride and satisfaction when she finally succeeded; the quivering of her bottom lip as she stood by our back door holding back tears before her first day of school; and the first time she randomly looked up at me with her beautiful blue eyes and said, "Daddy, I love you."

My emotions turned to fear, worry, and anger when my thoughts digressed to our unborn baby girl growing up, becoming a teenager, and eventually going on her first date. As any father will tell you, very few things incite fear, concern, and violence like the thought of a little heathen dating your precious little angel.

Not knowing what else I could do to address my concerns and that potential situation as I sat there in the hospital, I opened the laptop and ordered a Samurai sword from Japan called the "Guardian." Feeling relieved, I closed the laptop and my eyes and took a short rest.

Larn and I were both awakened by a nurse at sunrise. As the nurse was checking Larn's vitals, Larn looked over at me and asked, "Did you get any sleep at all?" I responded, "Very little, but I bought a Samurai sword." Larn gave me a puzzled look and asked me why in the world I bought a Samurai sword. When I explained that the purpose of the Samurai sword was to scare little boys that try to date our baby girl, Larn shook her head with what I interpreted as an understanding look on her face and informed me that worrying about our unborn daughter dating and buying weapons to protect her were probably a little premature and over-the-top. I agreed that the Samurai sword probably wasn't absolutely necessary given my hunting guns, bows, and knife collection, but I still believed it was a nice touch.

After monitoring Larn closely throughout the day, the nurses finally told her that it was time to push late in the afternoon. I was standing beside the bed holding Larn's hand and my breath when the doctor told her one more push. Seconds later, the doctor delivered our baby girl.

I stood with anticipation and excitement waiting to hear our daughter cry and for the doctor to hand our baby to Larn. Instead, the doctor frantically punched a button behind the bed, sirens went off, and people in scrubs filled the room. My anticipation and excitement immediately shifted to terror unlike anything I had ever experienced. I was helpless and feeling worthless as I stood there not knowing what else to do other than watch the commotion and try to convince Larn and myself that everything was fine.

As a herd of people in blue scrubs rushed out the door with our baby, Larn looked at me and pleaded, "Don't leave her." I was torn in half, not knowing whether to stay with Larn, who had just delivered our baby and was lying helpless in bed, or to go with our daughter as she was rushed out of the delivery room by strangers. Larn looked up at me with tears in her eyes and begged, "Please go with her – she needs you." I quickly kissed Larn and ran to catch up with doctors, nurses, and pharmacists that had our baby daughter.

After traversing a maze of halls and stairways, I raced through the back entrance to the neonatal intensive care unit. I quickly and thoroughly scrubbed my hands and ran to the back corner of the ICU where our daughter was lying as several doctors and nurses cared for her. As I stood over their shoulders watching, I asked the one question that I had to ask but was scared to death to know the answer to: "Is she going to be ok?" The doctor looked at me over her shoulder and said that they were doing everything they could, but that she would likely be fine. I was overwhelmed with tears and emotions as I sat down in the floor to catch my breath and slow the uncontrollable spinning of the world.

A little while later, Larn was rolled into the intensive care unit and we were able to hold our baby girl's hand for the first time. A few days later, we were allowed to lift her out of the hospital bed and hold her in our arms for the first time. A week or so later, our baby girl was released from intensive care. The afternoon after she was released, we arrived home with our healthy baby daughter.

Within the first few weeks after childbirth, we began to realize and understand the demands of parenthood. Every second that was not dedicated to the baby or working was spent cleaning or resting. Even if I had the time to fish or hunt, which I didn't, I wouldn't have been able to because I was still recovering from surgery on the torn rotator cuff.

The first few months passed in the blink of an eye. In what seemed like moments after we brought our baby girl home, it was time for her first Christmas. When we first discussed presents, I commented that our baby girl needed her own fishing rod. Larn was trying to gauge whether I was serious when she asked, "Do you really think a four month old needs her own rod?" Without hesitation, I responded "Absolutely!" A few weeks later, my newest fishing buddy received her first rod and reel, before she could walk, talk, crawl, or even sit-up.

Like father, like daughter!

When our daughter was a little over one, Larn and I began discussing the possibility of extending our family again. This time, we left the detailed planning and timeline to a much greater power. While we both hoped and prayed that we would be able to bring another healthy baby into the world, we fully understood and accepted that it was out of our hands.

Less than two months later, Larn commented that she was nauseated. A few minutes later, we both stood in utter shock looking at a plus sign on a home pregnancy test.

Throughout the pregnancy, Larn struggled with daily morning, afternoon, evening, and night sickness. Otherwise, the pregnancy generally went smoothly. We went together to each appointment and eagerly counted the days to the due date.

At a routine appointment a few weeks before the due date in early August, the doctor walked in and gave us the news that Larn's blood pressure was elevated again and that he thought it was best to induce labor early the following morning. We went home for the evening to make arrangements and prepare for the birth of our second daughter.

We drove to the hospital early the following morning and started the induction process. When the baby did not arrive by late afternoon, the doctor stopped the induction for the day and indicated that the nurses would restart the medications during the night.

We spent the rest of the night discussing our hopes, dreams, fears, and concerns. We were thrilled to welcome our baby into the world, but we both shared concerns about potential complications with the delivery.

After several hours of discussion, Larn told me that she was ready to sleep. I agreed and laid down on the hospital couch next to

Larn's bed. As she faded off to sleep, Larn looked over to me and commented, "I can't believe we will be responsible for another baby girl this time tomorrow." Her words yanked me back from the verge of sleep. I immediately set up on the couch as I tried to imagine our baby girl and the stubborn, independent, and beautiful little princess she would become.

My thoughts eventually strayed to our baby girl growing up and becoming a teenager and turned into worries and anger about a little boy wanting to date her one day. I immediately opened the laptop to find something to deter little boys from trying to date our youngest baby girl. I quickly found and ordered the perfect solution and found peace. I then closed the laptop and drifted off to sleep.

A few hours later, before sunrise, Larn and I were awakened by the nurse restarting the induction medicine. While the nurse was hanging the drip bag, Larn looked at me and asked in an accusatory and cynical tone, "What did you buy this time?" I chuckled and responded sheepishly, "A German longsword." Larn laughed, shook her head, and said, "It figures."

Later that day, I was standing beside the delivery bed holding Larn's hand as the nurses and the doctor encouraged her to push. When the nurse said, "One more push," a wave of excitement and pure terror flushed over me. I was horrified that the delivery of our baby girl would be immediately followed by sirens instead of crying, and I was completely helpless.

Moments later, Larn's final push was immediately followed by loud screaming as the doctor handed our healthy baby girl to Larn. We were both overwhelmed with tears and joy as we looked at our new beautiful daughter for the first time.

The nurse quickly grabbed the baby to check her vitals, weigh her, and swaddle her. As the nurse walked away, Larn struggled to keep her eyes open as she whispered, "We did good Daddy … I love you." I leaned over the bed, kissed her gently on the forehead, whispered, "Congratulations Mama," patted her shoulder, and then joked, "I'm going bear hunting now."

I have never seen anyone as exhausted as Larn was in that moment. I would have sworn that the simple task of opening her eyes would have tested the bounds of her strength and endurance. I would have been wrong. As soon as I made the joke about the bear, she clubbed me.

The following morning, our oldest daughter arrived at the hospital to meet her younger sister. As soon as our two-year-old walked in the room, she wanted in the bed to see her Mama and her baby "Sisty." I sat next to the bed with overwhelming pride and satisfaction as my beautiful wife held both of our two daughters together. For the first time, all three of my girls were together, and I could not have been prouder or happier.

She loves her baby "Sisty"

Two days later, we arrived home after being released from the hospital. We had foolishly read the internet and believed that adding a newborn to the established routine of a two-year-old would not be difficult. We also assumed that our second daughter would be the same as our first daughter. We were wrong on all accounts.

A few months later, Larn and I found ourselves in familiar waters as we discussed Christmas present ideas for our girls. Before I could even make the suggestion, Larn had written "fishing rod" on our youngest daughter's Christmas list. On Christmas morning, my newest and youngest fishing buddy held her first fishing rod and reel.

Trying to juggle two young babies and a busy work schedule is difficult. All of my time was devoted to family, working, or sleeping. While I still longed to hunt, fish, and spend time in the outdoors, my priorities were on family and career. The closest I came to spending time in the outdoors was watching the Outdoor Channel or the Sportsman's Network from the recliner with our daughters in my lap, which we did frequently.

During the summer, I tried several times to shoot my Mathews bow. Each time, I struggled because my draw length had changed as a result of shoulder surgery and drawing the bow back caused pain on the front of my shoulder.

I had desperately hoped to be ready to hunt on opening day of bow season. When opening day finally rolled around, I sat quietly at my desk wishing I was in a treestand.

I thought a lot about bow hunting following opening day and, the weekend following opening day, I made the decision that I really wanted a new bow. Larn and I were standing in the kitchen when I asked her if it was ok with her if I bought a new bow for my birthday.

In her usual supportive tone, she responded, "Absolutely." I then told Larn that I really wanted to get her a bow for my birthday too so that we could spend time together shooting and hunting. Larn loved the idea.

I was the first customer at the local archery shop the following Tuesday morning. After a lot of discussion and consideration, I picked out a Mathews bow for me and a Mission bow for Larn.

Two days later, I met Larn and the girls at the archery shop to set up Larn's bow. Within the first few shots, it became evident that Larn was going to be a crack shot with a bow.

Larn and I shot our bows together frequently at the family farm throughout the following spring and summer preparing for opening day of bow season. One of us would generally shoot while the other entertained our daughters. By early October, we were both shooting well and were ready for deer season.

Larn and I had sat in a double ladder stand on opening day and one other time during early bow season without seeing a deer. Larn thoroughly enjoyed spending time together in the outdoors, but it was evident that she really wanted to see a deer from the stand.

Later that month, on my birthday, we were sitting on stand again with our bows enjoying time together in the outdoors and hoping that a deer would walk by. A few hours into the afternoon hunt, there was a rustle to the left. We both looked up at the sound and, to both of our surprise, a wide eight-point buck materialized in the woods as he walked down a path that would bring him within twenty yards of the tree.

Larn stealthily grabbed her bow and quietly stood up in anticipation of the shot. With each passing moment, our anxiety grew as the buck walked down the trail that passed in front of the tree. Larn and I were both shaking and suffering from a severe case of buck fever when the buck finally stepped into Larn's range. Larn slowly shifted her feet, lifted her bow slightly over her head, drew back her string, anchored her knuckles in her cheek, looked through her peep sight, settled the pin on the buck's shoulder, and prepared to shoot.

Time came to a slow crawl in the moments leading up to the shot. Unfortunately, the shot didn't happen. As Larn stood there at full draw and prepared to squeeze the trigger of her release, something to the left of the tree unexpectedly spooked the buck. At the sound, he quickly walked to the right just out of range. As soon as the buck was out of range, Larn set back down to calm her nerves.

Larn and I were both upset that she had not gotten a shot on the buck. More importantly though, Larn had thoroughly enjoyed the thrill of bow hunting, and I had deeply enjoyed seeing the excitement and joy on Larn's face as she suffered from her first case of buck fever.

A few minutes later, we were both shocked when the buck stepped out again from behind the tree after circling back to where he had been spooked. As soon as Larn saw the buck, she once again grabbed her bow, slowly stood, shifted to her right, drew her bow back quietly, looked through her peep sight, and settled her pin just behind the left shoulder of the quartering away buck. With the confidence of an experienced life-long hunter, Larn slowly squeezed the trigger of her release.

Time once again came to a crawl as the cams on her Mission bow responded, the string released, and her arrow cleared the rest. The sound of her bow was immediately followed by a loud thump as her arrow hit true and buried behind the shoulder of the buck up to the pink and purple fletchings of her arrow. Larn made a perfect shot.

As Larn looked down the path where the deer had run, she began shaking uncontrollably. Her shaking was causing the tree to sway violently, which caused the few remaining leaves on the tree to fall to the ground.

After waiting about an hour, we climbed down to look for her deer. A few minutes later, we easily found her buck on the trail.

Larn's first deer with a bow

Larn was filled with pure excitement as we approached her first deer and sat down in the woods next to him. As I sat there, I thanked the buck, said a quick prayer, and took in every surreal moment.

On the afternoon of my birthday exactly one year after she first shot a bow, my wife and best friend made a perfect shot on an incredible buck with her bow. The hunt was perfect, my all-time favorite, and a day I will never forget. I couldn't imagine a better birthday.

When we told our daughters about their Mommy getting a deer with her bow, our oldest daughter made a big deal of the accomplishment and asked, "Dada, can I hunt with a bow too?" Moments later, I ordered her a camouflage shirt and an NXT Generation Bow from Amazon. Two days later, we were on a safari in our living room in full camo stalking the targets on our back door.

We spent countless hours shooting suction cup arrows at the door. Each time an arrow would stick to the glass, our daughter would scream "YES!" and we would celebrate.

Our youngest daughter was eager to bow hunt on the family safaris, and she often asked for her own bow. I had promised her that we would get her a bow when she was big enough to shoot her sister's bow.

Later the following year, our youngest daughter was finally able to shoot her sister's bow. She danced around the room yelling "YAY" when we told her that we were ordering her a bow. To our surprise, she abruptly stopped dancing and asked in her most serious voice, "Can it be pank?" We couldn't help but laugh as we ordered her a pink bow.

Since that day, Larn has traded in her Mission Bow for the Eva Shockey Bowtech bow, our oldest daughter has graduated to a red Mathews Genesis bow, our youngest daughter is still shooting her "pank" bow, and I "had" to buy another Mathews bow after another shoulder surgery.

Both of our daughters have also recently informed me that they need better fishing rods. When I asked them what they meant by "better," our oldest daughter said she really needs a Star Wars or Ninja Turtle rod, and our youngest daughter said she needs a rod with princesses instead of fairies.

I have promised both of our daughters that we will fish more this summer and that we will hunt for something other than the back door this fall. I have no doubt that they will hold me to my promise. I truly can't wait.

During my younger years, if anyone had ever asked me what I enjoyed most in life, I would have undoubtedly said fishing, hunting, and the outdoors. While I have deeply loved and appreciated every moment I have been blessed to spend in the woods and on the water, I have come to realize as I've gotten older that enjoying the outdoors has little to do with the catch or the kill and that the outdoors and the wonders of nature are far more special, enjoyable, fulfilling, and memorable when experienced with friends and loved ones. I can't think of anywhere I would rather be than spending time in the outdoors, especially with my girls.

My Girls

Acknowledgments

As I sit here 30,000 feet above the ground flying between Saskatchewan and home after a week of bear hunting and walleye fishing, I cannot help but reflect on everyone that has made this book possible. I am truly grateful for every person that has influenced me and been a part of my life. From the bottom of my heart – Thank You! I would not be here today without you.

I would also like to take this opportunity to say a few special thanks.

First, I would like to truly thank God for the blessings, opportunities, and lessons. Nothing would be possible without Him.

To Mom and Dad, thank you for giving me the freedom to make mistakes and for trusting that I would make good decisions. I am honored and humbled to be your son.

To Sunni, thank you for being such an incredible sister, friend, mentor, and role model. You will never know how much you mean to me and how much of an influence you have had on my life.

To all that were mentioned in the book, thank you for the memories, the friendship, and everything that you have done for me. I love and appreciate you all!

To my good friend Clark, thank you for inspiring me, encouraging me, and for helping with the book. I appreciate everything you have done to make this book what it is today.

To Drew, the fishing nut and the best outdoor photographer I know, thank you for all of your help with the book and for taking the incredible picture on the cover. You are a great friend and an incredible fisherman.

To Archer, FL, Ryan, Craig, Paul, Dale, little Cuz, Trav, Jeremy, Trace, Ozzie, Big Shooter, Dee, Bayless, and anyone else that has wet a line or walked the woods with me, thank you for the brotherhood, the fellowship, and for all of the memories and experiences. You are and will always be a part of me.

To Greg with Big Mac Publishers, thank you for believing in me and my stories and for helping me realize the dream of publishing a book.

To Jackie Bushman, Bill Dance, Hank Parker, Tom Miranda, Jim Shockey, and all the other outdoorsmen that I watched on TV and read about in magazines, thank you for the inspiration and instruction, for giving me ideas for my bucket list, and for helping me dream beyond the woods and water of North Alabama.

To Sara Lee, thank you for making that exotic microwave dinner that inspired me over breakfast many years ago.

Last but definitely not least, to my girls, Larn, El Brooke, and Kibbers, thank you for being the best family this boy from Alabama could ever hope and pray for. I love you more than you will ever know!

Until next time, may you all have tight lines and favorable winds!

Corey

About the Author

Corey Jenkins

Corey Jenkins was born and raised in Hartselle, a small town in North Alabama. After graduating from Hartselle High School, he left home and earned his B.S. in Computer Science from the University of Alabama at Birmingham. He completed this degree as quickly as possible, graduating in just over three years. Realizing that he had been in a hurry to graduate for no apparent reason, Corey then attended Cumberland School of Law and earned his Juris Doctorate. Continuing his quest to be an eternal student, he then moved to Gainesville, Florida to earn his LL.M. in taxation from the law school at the University of Florida.

Upon finishing his formal education, he moved back to North Alabama to practice corporate and tax law. His decision to move home was based largely on his overwhelming desire to return to the woods and waters where he grew up hunting and fishing. He introduced his wife Lauren to the outdoors of his youth, and they now spend time hunting, fishing, and enjoying the outdoors with their two daughters.

Through the years, Corey has won numerous awards and received countless accolades, the most important of which include: (1) winning the Plano Junior Alabama State Bass Fishing Championship at fifteen;

Junior Alabama State Bass Fishing Championship at fifteen

(2) being named in the top 100 non-professional typists in the country at seventeen;

(3) receiving a large first place trophy for winning a putt-putt tournament in high school (which he still proudly displays to this day);

(4) winning a bottle of champagne that he was too young to drink at a skeet shooting tournament off the back of a cruise ship at seventeen by hitting thirty straight clays (he also still keeps the bottle of champagne to this day, unopened); and

(5) receiving the "Dad of the Year" award from his daughters for several consecutive years.

While Corey's extensive bucket list has evolved over time, writing a book has been a mainstay on the list ... until now.

Lines, Tines & Southern Pines is Corey's first book. For more information or to contact Corey, please visit his Amazon author page, or www.linestinespines.com.

In Loving Memory of PawPaw

Glossary
Understanding the Local Lexicon

Realizing that many of the terms and phrases used throughout the foregoing chapters are slang, unusual, specific to the outdoors, or unique to the South (or, more narrowly, North Alabama), I figured it may be helpful to understand the meaning of certain terms and phrases, at least through my eyes:

"Allen wrench" is the wrench you use to adjust virtually all screws on a bow. It is also known as a hex key. Unfortunately, Allen wrenches come in many different sizes, and you never seem to have the size you are looking for when you need it.

"Anchoring" generally refers to whatever an archer does to replicate his or her routine to ensure shot consistency. I anchor my arrow nock to the side of my mouth and I anchor my right thumb into a little groove on the back of my neck. These have been my "anchors" since Steve taught me how to shoot a bow many years ago.

"Arrow nock" is the part of the arrow that attaches to the bow string. Anytime I shoot bows with friends, I usually end up aiming at their arrow nocks moreso than bullseyes. It adds a level of entertainment and frustration, depending on who is the better shot.

"Baitcaster" refers to a horizontal reel that is engaged with your thumb. Baitcasters are generally considered to be substantially more difficult to throw than "spinning reels" or "Zebcos," primarily because baitcasters occasionally blow up (commonly referred to as a backlash or bird's nest) when cast. These blow ups render the reel unusable until you untangle or cur your line. Fish will undoubtedly bust all around the boat while you are fixing a backlash and then mysteriously stop as soon as you are ready to cast again.

"*Bassmaster*" refers to the magazine by that name. I have read *Bassmaster* magazine as long as I can remember, and it has always been one of my favorite publications.

"Bead of a shotgun" refers to the little bead on the end of the barrel of a shotgun. To aim a shotgun, you need to look down the barrel, preferably without resting your face on the gun, and use the bead to aim at your target.

"Bear" means Paul William "Bear" Bryant, the former head coach of the Alabama Crimson Tide and generally considered the greatest football coach to ever walk the face of the planet. Anyone that argues otherwise generally has little credibility, unless they are arguing that Nick Saban is the greatest coach of all time (which leads to interesting discussions).

"Beast" is a very difficult term to define. It can refer to anything that is abnormally large, such as "that fish is a beast" or "look over at that deer, he's a beast." It can also refer to something that is dangerous, such as "that ravenous dog is really dangerous, he's a beast." The term beast can also refer to someone that is extremely good at what he does, such as "every running back to play for Alabama over the last five to ten years has been a complete beast." How do you know when something or someone is a beast? To quote former United States Supreme Court Justice Stewart when describing how to tell if something is pornography, "I know it when I see it."

"Bedding area" is an area where deer congregate when not feeding or traveling. Bedding areas are typically thick areas that provide hiding places for deer and a sanctuary from predators and hunters.

"Best spot on the property" is the best spot to hunt or fish and is generally where you will find me. Several friends of mine joke that if I ever tell you what to do and then I do something else, ignore what I say and do what I'm doing.

"Better hunting land" is a vague and amorphous concept that is akin to the saying "the grass is always greener on the other side." The phrase "better hunting land" generally means a hunting area that, for one reason or another, you believe is better than where you are hunting. It can refer to completely different states (like saying that Iowa, Illinois, and Kentucky have better hunting land than North Alabama). It can also refer to a different stand on the land where you are hunting. Anytime you hunt somewhere and don't see deer, you can pretty well guarantee anywhere else would have been "better hunting land."

"Bill Dance" is one of the two fishermen I remember watching on TV and reading about more than any other fisherman growing up. If I wasn't fishing or hunting on a Saturday morning, I was sitting in front of the TV watching "Bill Dance Outdoors." Many kids want to be athletes when they grow up. I wanted to fish.

"Birmingham" is the largest city in Alabama, located approximately 90 miles south of Huntsville, 60 miles south of Hartselle, 90 miles north of Montgomery, 60 miles northeast of Tuscaloosa, and 250 miles north of Mobile.

"Blooded" generally refers to the rite of passage when someone kills his or her first deer. What is involved in being blooded varies depending on groups and geographic areas. When I was a child, being "blooded" was first explained to me as a Native American tradition intended to honor the animal and recognize the hunter coming of age. I have explained the tradition to every person that has ever shot his or her first deer with me, and I only recall one person ever asking not to be blooded (and he wasn't). Larn was blooded when she shot her first deer.

"Bomber" refers to a specific type of crankbait that has an "A" shaped bill. Bomber crankbaits are also often referred to as "Model A's."

"Bore site" is the initial process of adjusting your scope to be as close as possible to zeroed, typically with the assistance of a laser or light.

"Bow" is a general term that refers to a weapon that shoots arrows. When I refer to bows, I am generally referring to compound bows (*i.e.,* a bow that is held vertically and that has wheels or cams on the end to guide the string). Many archers use traditional bows (*i.e.,* a longbow or a recurve). On the other end of the spectrum is a crossbow (which is generally shot using a trigger like a gun instead of releasing a string like the other bows). All bows are effective and fun, but most people are loyal to one specific type (and are confident their version is either the best or the purest).

"Breaking of bow cam or wheel" refers to when the string of a compound bow is pulled back past the point where the cam or wheel rolls over and the string becomes much easier to hold (*i.e.,* letoff).

"Broadhead" is the razor sharp arrow tip that is used while hunting with a bow. Broadheads come in many different shapes and sizes. I have scars on both of my hands from screwing in broadheads, removing broadheads, or sharpening broadheads.

"*Buckmasters*" is the hunting magazine and television show that I remember watching most when I was younger. I used to fantasize about hunting in exotic locations alongside Jackie Bushman with Buckmasters. I learned many things watching and reading *Buckmasters* and still enjoy it to this day.

"Busting" refers to fish coming to the surface, often to eat baitfish; attack a bird, frog, or another animal; or, more often than not, taunt the fisherman.

"Charburger" is a little hamburger restaurant on Highway 69 near Guntersville. A Wildcat Cheeseburger and a strawberry shake from the Charburger was a delicacy growing up.

"Clicks" refers to the little lines on the knobs on a scope. Moving a scope "a click" generally means that you move the point of impact one-quarter of an inch at 100 yards, at least in most hunting scopes.

"Crack shot" means someone that shoots extremely well and generally doesn't miss. I have claimed to be a crack shot numerous times, but rarely actually been one.

"Crankbait" means a specific type of fishing lure that has a "lip" or "bill" that causes the lure to go deeper when pulled.

"Cricket tube" refers to anything that you use to hold crickets to go fishing. Most cricket tubes are wire with red or yellow tops, with one side angled to make it easy to remove a single cricket for bait. I've also had cricket tubes that were cardboard boxes and looked nothing like a tube.

"Cross ties" are the wood pieces that you see between the tracks on the railroad. When I was a kid, we had a few old cross ties in our back yard underneath the plum tree.

"Crybaby Holler" is an area near Hartselle that many believe is haunted. According to legend (at least as I've always heard it), a baby died in the hollow many years ago and, if you drive over the bridge, your car will shake, you will hear a baby crying, and other crazy things happen. It is a very odd place. However, I can honestly say, going through Crybaby Holler to try to catch fish isn't anywhere near the craziest thing I've done to try to catch fish, even at four.

"Cullman" means the city in Alabama between Hartselle and Birmingham, between exit 310 and 299 on Interstate 65. PawPaw's farm was just outside of Cullman, in Vinemont.

"Deliar scale" is a brand of fish scale that generally had a reputation for being accurate. I rarely agreed with the scale and always hated it.

"Double ladder stand" refers to a type of stand that has a single ladder but two seats, often 16-20 feet up a tree.

"Dove field" refers to any field that you hunt hoping for dove. I've hunted many dove fields where I only saw crows and other birds that weren't doves. It was still a dove field.

"Draw a string back" or "draw a bow" means to pull back a bow string to prepare for a shot.

"Exotic Sara Lee" means any Sara Lee dinner that you are eating in a pinch. Exotic Sara Lee can help hunger and provide inspiration for a book.

"Eye of the Tiger" refers to the song from Rocky. I challenge any person to watch the part of any Rocky movie where Eye of the Tiger is being played and not get chill bumps. It is truly not possible.

"Fishing hole" means any spot that you fish. A fishing hole can refer to a spot hundreds of miles offshore or a bank on the edge of a small stream. There is no science behind it – a fishing hole is anywhere you fish.

"Flint Creek" is a creek off of the Tennessee River that runs alongside the Refuge near Hartselle and Flint (now part of Decatur).

"Flip the bail" refers to flipping over the top part of a spinning reel so that the line can freely come unspooled.

"Foolproof hunting gadget" means the latest and greatest thing that is guaranteed to help you see and kill more and bigger deer. I've never found a hunting gadget that worked, but yet I still buy them every single year.

"Grandmother" refers to Dad's mom. In Alabama, there are only a handful of names that are generally used to refer to grandparents. My grandmother on my Dad's side just happened to be "Grandmother."

"Granny" refers to Mom's mom. Granny is buried next to PawPaw. She loved her family and Alabama football more than anything. She kinda looked like Yoda.

"Green bucket" refers to a five-gallon bucket that has been painted green and that is used as a seat while dove hunting. Obvious … yes. Terribly uncomfortable … most definitely. More affordable than a camouflage seat ... absolutely.

"Guntersville" refers to Lake Guntersville, the best largemouth bass fishing lake in the country, at least in my opinion.

"Hank Parker" refers to one of my two favorite fishermen growing up. Meeting Hank Parker and getting his autograph during high school was one of the highlights of my teenage years. I still catch myself singing the theme song of his show occasionally.

"Hartselle" is where Larn and I were born and raised. Unless you are from there or have family there, keep up with high school baseball in Alabama, like to antique shop, need gas around mile marker 328 on Interstate 65, or are lost, you probably have never been there. I still love Hartselle, and part of me will always consider Hartselle home.

"Hawg" refers to a large bass. Other common terms include: Lunker, Toad, Pig, Monster, Giant Greenhead, and anything else that comes to mind when you first see a big bass.

"Highway 69" refers to Highway 69 in Alabama, particularly the stretch of the highway between Cullman and Guntersville.

"Horsepower" is the measurement used to determine the size of the motor on a boat. As a child, I always questioned why the size of a boat's motor was measured in horsepower since horses are very slow swimmers.

"Hunting camp" means anywhere that you hunt if you stay overnight.

"Jim 'N Nick's BBQ" is a restaurant that now has several locations in Alabama. After Larn and I decided to get married, she joked that I was the only guy ever brave enough to take her to a barbecue restaurant, since her Dad owns Southern Hickory Barbecue. I definitely prefer the barbecue at Southern Hickory Barbecue, but I love the chicken fingers, lemon pie, and sweet tea at Jim 'N Nick's.

"Jon boat" is a short, narrow, and uncomfortable metal boat. A Jon boat is virtually always green.

"Livewell" is the compartment in bass boats that holds water and has pumps and aerators to keep fish alive.

"Log" means anything that (1) is underwater; (2) you can't see; and (3) your lure is hung on. Rocks, trees, and old rope are all often logs.

"Mess of fish" means the exact amount of fish that you need for a meal. The number of fish that constitutes a "mess" is always uncertain and generally means the lesser of the most fish you can catch or the amount of fish you need to feed everyone you expect to eat dinner, plus two.

"Minnow bucket" means a container that is used to store "minners" and similar live bait. Like cricket tubes, minnow buckets come in all shapes and sizes.

"Monster" has a meaning very similar to "beast." The term monster can just as easily apply to a large fish, a mature buck, or a ravenous predator stalking its prey. A monster can be many things. You'll know it when you see it.

"Northport" is the town just north of Tuscaloosa.

"PawPaw" is Mom's dad. Grandfathers in the South can be referred to by a multitude of names, although PawPaw, Pop, Paw, Papa, and other similar names are most prevalent. Our daughter's refer to Larn's dad as PawPaw. They struggle understanding that their PawPaw is different from my PawPaw.

"Peep site" means a small piece that you attach to a bow string that has a little hole that you look through after you pull back a bow. A peep site helps you anchor to the same spot and shoot consistently.

"Point buck" refers to the number of separate points on a Buck's antlers or "rack." For example, a buck that has eight points is an eight-point buck. Funny thing is that the number of points doesn't really define the size of a deer. For example, a six-point can be a lot bigger than a ten-point. Given this, some hunters focus on "score" of a buck, which is based on the total number of inches of antler as opposed to the number of points.

"Piggly Wiggly" is a grocery store that was once extremely popular in North Alabama. A few still exist, but they are generally in rural areas now. Walking into a Piggly Wiggly today is like going back in time. I still love going into "The Pig" as Dad always called it.

"Pin" refers to a site on a bow. Typically, a bow site will have multiple pins that are zeroed at different ranges (such as ten yards, twenty yards, and thirty yards). Pins today are generally fiberoptic and extremely easy to see. Pins when I started bow hunting were generally gold and painted with Mom's fingernail polish (when she wasn't looking).

"Pinch point" refers to an area that deer generally gravitate to or are forced to travel because of natural terrain or some other factor.

"Plane" is when a boat levels off near parallel to the water after the initial acceleration. Boats don't plane the same way. Dad and I fished in an old ski boat for several years that wouldn't plane unless one of us jumped up and down in the front of the boat. We got some incredible looks and laughs boating down Lake Guntersville with one us jumping frantically in the front of the boat.

"Pound test line" is some mythical strength test that is intended to correlate to the strength and diameter of fishing line. I tested multiple different lines once to see how close the pound ratings were. I almost dropped a ten-pound weight on my foot and lost an eye. I decided to leave it to the experts.

"Pounding the same area" means you are fishing or hunting the same spots over and over. If it aint broke, why fix it?

"Pull up a bow" means the process of pulling a bow from the ground to a tree in a stand using a "tow rope" attached to the bow and the stand."

"Quiver" is the part of the bow that holds arrows. I used a 3 arrow quiver until I shot every arrow out of the quiver one day (as described in Doe Fever). After that day, I swapped to a larger quiver. Funny, I haven't shot more than one arrow out of my quiver again out of a stand.

"Rat-L-Trap" is a flat crankbait without the "lip" or "bill." Rat-L-Trap was a specific brand of "lipless crankbait" made by Bill Lewis.

"Real American" refers to the introduction music used by Hulk Hogan during the earlier years of his career, before he joined the New World Order.

"Realtree" is one of the most popular camouflage patterns. During the years when I hunted the Refuge, I wore Realtree exclusively. To this day, I still like to wear Realtree camo.

"Release" is a mechanical device that connects to a bow string or a loop on a bow string and that is held by the archer while drawing back a bow. A release has a trigger and is used in lieu of your fingers.

"Rut" means the period during deer season when deer breed. Deer rut at different times depending on geographic location and other factors (including moon phase, weather, and genetics). Many hunters consider the week leading up to rut to be the best time to hunt.

"Scouting" means the process of trying to locate deer or areas where deer are traveling. We would often end up scouting during morning hunts, especially when it was cold and we couldn't stand sitting still in a tree.

"Secret lure" means the go-to lure that you have the most confidence in under the circumstances.

"Set the hook" is the process of "jerking" or "yanking" a rod back to bury the hooks in a fish's mouth past the barb to make sure the fish is hooked solid. You can also set the hook in other things, like logs and jaws.

"Settle the pin" means the process where you try to calm your nerves enough to hold the pin on a bow relatively steady so that you can hit what you are aiming at.

"Shooter buck" is a buck that the hunter considers big or mature enough to shoot. What constitutes a shooter buck is different depending on the hunter. To some hunters, a shooter is any deer that walks out. I personally subscribe to the theory that it is better to harvest older deer to let the younger deer grow up.

"Shooting house" is a type of stand that has four walls, a roof, and windows. A shooting house protects the hunter from the elements pretty well, but also limits the ability to hear the surroundings.

"Southern Hickory Barbecue" is a barbecue restaurant that has separate stores in Hartselle, Cullman, and Arab. I grew up eating barbecue from Southern Hickory and still enjoy it to this day.

"Spinnerbaits" is a type of lure that has a wire that makes a V, with a hook on one side and a piece of metal that spins on the other side. Dad always hated spinnerbaits, so I had to pick them up on my own (and by watching Hank Parker).

"Spinning rod" means a type of rod that holds a spinning reel. Spinning reels are generally easier to throw than a baitcaster and not quite as accurate, at least to me. Spinning reels are also better than baitcasters for lighter lures or if you want to skip lures under or into cover.

"Stand" means anything that you sit in or on to deer hunt. A stand can include a fixed platform with a ladder, a seat and base that you use to climb a tree, or a shooting house.

"Stocking a pond" means putting fish in a pond. Those fish can be babies (or fingerlings) or fish you "borrowed" from your neighbor's pond.

"Summit stand" is a specific brand of treestand that I have always used. I still use two separate Summit stands.

"Texas-rigged worm" is a way to rig a worm where your line is threaded through a weight that looks like a bullet, and the bullet sits directly on the worm.

"Tine" is another word for a sharp point on a deer's antler.

"Trash fish" means any fish that you aren't fishing for or that your friend catches.

"Trim the motor" means moving a motor up or down. Generally, the motor is trimmed all the way down at takeoff (which results in a quick plane). Once the boat is on plane, the motor is trimmed up. The more the motor is trimmed, the faster the boat goes.

However, there is a point where the ride of a boat becomes extremely rough if a motor is trimmed up too high.

"Troll" means throwing lures behind a boat and letting the speed of the boat work the lures.

"Trophy bass" is any bass that is a trophy. The definition of a trophy varies between fishermen. In my view, any largemouth bass over seven pounds is a trophy (with any fish over nine pounds being an absolute monster and any fish over ten pounds being a fish of a lifetime), and any smallmouth bass over five pounds is a trophy (with any fish over six pounds being an absolute monster and any fish over seven pounds being a fish of a lifetime).

"Tuscaloosa" is the city where the University of Alabama is located. See above definition of Birmingham for more information on geography.

"Went together" meant that you called each other boyfriend and girlfriend, at least in Hartselle.

"Woods come to life" is the period just after daybreak when the fog lifts, it seems like a switch is flipped, and birds and animals materialize from nowhere.

"WWF" now means the World Wildlife Fund. However, back in the day (which is also a phrase that is commonly used in North Alabama), WWF means the World Wrestling Federation.

"Zebco" refers to a brand of rod and reel. I believe every rod and reel ever owned by PawPaw was a Zebco. In fact, I believe more Zebcos have been purchased than any other brand rod and reel. I gave away my last Zebco a few years ago to a kid that was interested in learning how to fish. There will always be a fond place in my heart for Zebcos.

"Zero" generally means the process of adjusting the sites of a bow or gun to be accurate. Likewise, a gun or bow that is "zeroed" is accurate. In order to zero a rifle, you typically attach the scope to the rifle, bore site it, place paper at a short distance to make sure you are close to the bullseye, and then extend the range of the target while adjusting the site.

".270" refers to a popular caliber deer rifle.

"7mm-08" is another popular deer rifle and is preferred by hunters that shoot under 200 yards and don't like guns that "kick" a lot. I like to make fun of Charlie 2 Shot for using a 7mm-08. Not because there is anything wrong with the gun, but because I like making fun of him.

www.ingramcontent.com/pod-product-compliance
Lightning Source LLC
LaVergne TN
LVHW051122080426
835510LV00018B/2180